We rejoice whenever we find the truth and, surely it is found in this insightful book by Frank Retief. Here is a clear, concise presentation of the saving gospel of Jesus Christ that is faithful to Scripture and accessible and readable to all. You will certainly want to devour the message of this work and carefully consider your own life and where you find yourself with the Lord. More than this, you will want to give this book to others. Whether you are already a believer, desiring the comfort and assurance of your own salvation, or an unbeliever needing to yet come to faith in Christ, I commend this book to you and the clear, biblical instruction of its pages.

Steven J. Lawson
Senior Pastor, Christ Fellowship Baptist Church, Teaching Fellow,
Ligonier Ministries, Mobile, Alabama

Enquirers and believers alike will find in Frank Retief's compelling style and luminous stories a readily-constructible platform for a credible Christian world-view. Further; these thirteen chapters – each concluding with Bible passages and study-guide questions – provide a perfect answer for churches on the look-out for a highly satisfying group study course.

Richard Bewes OBE
Former Rector of All Souls Church, Langham Place, London

This small book does two great things. It gets into the heart of the Christian gospel because Frank Retief knows his Bible. And it gets into the hearts of fearful people because Frank Retief knows the real world. As he takes the Word of a faithful God to the needs of uncertain people he provides straight and comforting answers. I hope this gets into the hands of thousands.

Simon Manchester
St Thomas' Anglican Church, North Sydney

Safe? helpfully moves the Christian looking for assurance beyond his or her own feelings into the trustworthy Word of God. It will benefit any reader looking to understand what God has done for us in Christ and how He gives peace and comfort to God's people. You will want to keep copies of this clear, faithful, and pastorally sensitive book on hand to give away to others.

Michael McKinley
Senior Pastor, Guildford Baptist Church, Sterling, Virginia

For many years I chaired a Christian convention in Sydney, Australia, in all that time I have never seen Australians respond to a speaker in the way they responded to Frank Retief. Frank is a gifted evangelist, clear and succinct! I warmly commend this book, focusing on the gospel and highlighting the greatest of great truths, justification. You will read it to your benefit and think of many friends who will be helped as well.

David Cook
Formerly Principal, Sydney Missionary and Bible College, Sydney

Frank Retief is rightly honoured throughout his native South Africa and elsewhere for his winsome ministry of the Word of God and for his enviable ability to convey deep biblical truths in a way that clarifies the mind and gladdens the heart. These qualities shine through every page of this delightful book, in which he focusses on the theme of Christian assurance in the Letter to the Romans. I can think of nothing better to give to new converts — or to be read by believers who are not crystal clear about their eternal security.

John Blanchard
Internationally-known Christian preacher, apologist and author, Surrey

Safe?

How we can be sure of God's love

FRANK RETIEF

Unless otherwise indicated, all Scripture quotations are taken from the *Holy Bible New International Version*. Copyright © 1973, 1978, 1984 by International Bible Society. Used by permission of Hodder & Stoughton Publishers, a member of the Hodder Headline Group. All rights reserved. NIV is a registered trademark of International Bible Society. UK trademark number 1448790.

Scripture quotations marked ESV are from *The Holy Bible, English Standard Version*, copyright © 2001 by Crossway Bibles, a division of Good News Publishers. Used by permission. All rights reserved. ESV Text Edition: 2007.

Frank Retief is the Bishop of the Church of England in South Africa, author, expositor and international conference speaker.

Copyright © Frank Retief 2012

ISBN 978-1-84550-970-5

10 9 8 7 6 5 4 3 2 1

Published in 2012
by
Christian Focus Publications, Ltd
Geanies House, Fearn,
Ross-shire, IV20 1TW, Scotland
www.christianfocus.com

Cover design by Daniel van Straaten

Printed by Nørhaven, Denmark

CONTENTS

Introduction

Becoming a Christian is meant to produce peace and joy, yet this is not always the experience of the believer. Why not? Most often it is because we have failed to grasp the true meaning and extent of the gospel message.

This book is designed to help those people who have truly received Christ as their Saviour but are confused by the feeling that nothing seems to have changed. Are you one of them? Most people gauge the reality of their conversion by the way they feel. For some people becoming a Christian is such a momentous event that the sense of being pardoned and inwardly renewed often results in joy and relief and a sense of belonging. But this emotional adrenaline has to solidify into a rugged understanding of the gospel or it will leave the new believer bewildered when the feelings wane. On the other hand some people become Christians in a progressive and un-emotional way and they may sometimes wonder if anything real and lasting has happened to them.

Many Christians are ignorant about how they are supposed to feel from day to day. The ordinary burdens of living in a fallen and sinful world descend on them and they no longer feel good or victorious. Instead they often feel guilty and confused. There are sometimes huge emotional expectations about the moment of commitment to Christ. When these don't materialise, some people commence a fruitless search for spiritual thrills. This can lead to perpetual disillusionment or even weird and wrong teaching. Such people often end up in the arms of strange and fanatical groups on the periphery of Christianity.

I urge you to avoid that. If you are feeling spir-itually dry and barren, let me assure you that the answer lies primarily in understanding the enor-mousness of what happens to those who turn to Christ. I do not mean to suggest that feelings are not important or that nothing should be experienced in the realm of the emotions. Far from it! I mere-ly want to point out that feelings are the result of other input into our lives – especially our minds. To use computer jargon, if the input is wrong, the print-out will be wrong. But if the input is right, the results will be right.

Feelings are so easily manipulated and changed. We are fallen people and part of the effect of our fallenness and imperfection is seen in the change-ability of our feelings and the ease with which they can play havoc with us.

We need to make sure that our information is correct, that we understand the privileges of believing the gospel. If we understand these privileges, then I say unhesitatingly that, regardless of the ups and downs of life, we can and should have blessed assurance.

I

How bad is the bad news?

To have real inner joy and peace as a Christian, it is imperative to understand from what we have been rescued. Sin is an awesome power that affects every part of our lives.

Paul quotes from two Old Testament psalms to describe the human situation – Psalm 14:1-3 and Psalm 53:1-3. He combines these two verses in Romans 3:10-18 to give us a grim and terrible picture of men and women without God. Consider the following statement:

> There is no-one righteous, not even one.
> (Rom. 3:10)

This is a profound statement that clearly contradicts the way the world thinks today. We often hear that criminal offenders merely need education or rehabilitation to cease their antisocial behaviour and it is probably true that they would benefit greatly from various forms of education and social work. But the Bible states with bold simplicity that the real problem is that, by nature, people are not righteous. This means that we do not automatically seek to do what is right. We are wrong on the inside.

A statement like this may sound strange in these days when there is a high level of awareness about the devastation of war, the injustices of racism and bigotry, the ruining of the environment and other great global concerns. In the face of the massive problems that confront our world, it may seem very old fashioned and even strange to talk about being righteous or unrighteous on a personal level.

It may help us to understand this statement if we realise that the Bible does not teach that we are incapable of doing anything good or noble, nor does it suggest that we do not often attempt to do so. Rather we are to understand that the Bible is measuring us against the standard of God's righteousness and His laws. Good and noble as many of our deeds may be, the truth is that we are not righteous in all things. Our tendency is to unrighteousness. Hatred, war, destruction and pragmatic morality are the things that characterise us. We embrace what is expedient and satisfies our lusts, our moods and our conscience. Even if we are not guilty of great violence or immorality, there is one sin that holds us all in its deadly grip – the sin of pride. Pride is a refusal to acknowledge that we have any spiritual need; a rejection of God's Word and His assessment of us; and a hardening of our hearts towards HIM.

Let's go further:

> There is no-one who understands, no-one who seeks God. (Rom. 3:11)

In the Bible the word 'understanding' usually refers to a spiritual understanding or insight into the character and the ways of God. By nature we have no such understanding. Instead we are creatures of darkness and our thoughts about life's values and about what is right and wrong are futile.

Seeking God means a wholehearted determination to live for Him. It means that we will seek His will and obey Him in all things. It means we want to recognise Him as the ruler of the world and we want Him to rule over us. We are not like that by nature. Instead, although we may have plenty of religious instinct, the pure worship of the true God is something far removed from us. We are, in fact, enemies of God.

> All have turned away, they have together become worthless; there is no-one who does good, not even one. (Rom. 3:12)

The thoughts of verses ten and eleven are underscored in this verse, but there are additional thoughts.

Firstly, 'all have turned away'. The action is ours. We deliberately turn away from goodness, righteousness and godliness. Secondly, 'they have together become worthless'. This does not mean that people, even unrighteous people, are worthless as human beings. Rather, in terms of a relationship to God, their efforts at religion and worship, their lifestyles, values, thoughts and actions are utterly worthless.

> Their throats are open graves; their tongues practise deceit. The poison of vipers is on their lips.
> (Rom. 3:13)

The first three verses above (Rom. 3:10-12) describe our character without God. The following verses (Rom. 3:13-18) describe the consequences of living without righteousness and understanding. These consequences usually take the form of broken relationships, and broken relationships often begin with bad communication between people.

'Their throats are open graves' means that we speak death to each other. The stench of decay enters our communication.

'Their tongues practise deceit' indicates that we are not honest or truthful. Often the pride we take in what we like to describe as our honesty and straight talk disguises insensitivity to others.

'... the poison of vipers is on their lips' suggests that we adopt the cunning of a snake, the slipperiness of a serpent in our dealings with each other. This is the consequence of broken relationships in terms of our dealings and communication with each other.

> Their mouths are full of cursing and bitterness.
> (Rom. 3:14)

Many a man and woman can bear testimony to the truth of these words. Cursing and bitterness are the rock bottom of human relationships. This is the logical next step – in a world that does not know God, people cannot live at peace with one another.

> Their feet are swift to shed blood ... (Rom. 3:15)

Violence. Think of this reference to violence for a moment. Is it not a picture of our world? There is a lack of righteousness and integrity. Many actions, promises, plans and conferences are worthless. Acrimony, lying, deceit, corruption, bribery, and international treaties are not worth the time and effort spent making them, let alone the paper they are written on – these characterise society. Finally, we have bombs, bullets, batons and bloodshed.

This may well reflect the state, not only of our world, but also of the homes in which we live. Tension, strife and self-centeredness may have given way to verbal and even physical violence. Note the next verse:

> … ruin and misery mark their ways, and the way of peace they do not know. (Rom. 3:16-17)

Many reading these words would have to say, 'That is how it was with me'. Their lives were marked by ruin, misery and the absence of peace. Why? Because there was a time when:

> There is no fear of God before their eyes.
> (Rom. 3:18).

That is the world without God, the condition of every man and woman without God. That is the picture, the misery and failure of our world and our society. The bad news is really bad. Without God, we are in a hopeless situation. That is the way with every person who does not know Jesus Christ personally, and that is the way it once was with every person who is now a Christian.

You may have many struggles as a Christian, but pause for a moment to consider what you were before you met Christ as your Saviour.

Study Questions

Read Romans 3:9-18.

1. Do you think this is a realistic picture of human nature or do you think Paul is exaggerating?
    Refer to:

    *   Psalm 51:5
    *   Psalm 58:3
    *   John 8:44
    *   Romans 3:23

2. If the scripture verses referred to above do reflect a true picture of human nature, why is everybody not as bad as it is possible to be?
    Discuss the role of:

    *   Natural restraints upon us
    *   The restraints placed upon us by society
    *   The restraints of temperament

3. Discuss the following two sentences in terms of family, friends and workplace:

    *   Our sinfulness is seen primarily in refusing to recognise God's rule over us.
    *   Our broken relationship with God is reflected in our broken relationships with each other.

4. If you were suddenly called into the presence of God, how acceptable do you think you would be?

    - Totally acceptable
    - Fairly acceptable
    - Totally unacceptable

    Why did you answer the way you did?

2

God's solution

What is the only thing God can do with rebels like us? It's simple. He has to punish us. This statement has a 'cringe' factor built into it. The idea of 'punishment' in our world today sounds crude, old fashioned and brutal.

I want you to enter the blessed assurance of knowing that God loves you and accepts you, but you cannot do that until you have seen the seriousness of your condition and the greatness of God's grace. I also need to say at this point that there are no short cuts to assurance of salvation. There is no quick fix. You have to take the trouble to think through these issues. I can offer you no clever slogans to make you feel good. You must follow the biblical argument if you want to know the boundless joy of being sure that you are God's child.

Think for a moment. This sinful condition of ours makes it impossible for God to bless us and accept us unconditionally. Why? Because God is different; He is not like us. Sometimes the Bible uses words and phrases that are not normally part of our vocabulary. Among the many words used to describe God in the Bible, let me mention two.

The first is **holy**. This means that there is no evil in God. He is incapable of evil in any shape or form. The second word is **righteousness**. This means that everything God does is always right, even if we cannot understand it or fathom it. He is incapable of engaging in any action which is wrong. Another word is **just**. God is perfect and amongst His perfections is His justice. This means that God can and must always react to that which is wrong. We all depend on God being just even if we do not realise it. Because we are created in His image we instinctively want justice to prevail in our world. And we are outraged when it does not. We need God to be holy, righteous and just.

But we are not like that. In fact, we are the exact opposite. We are not holy; we are basically evil. We are not all as wicked as it is possible to be, but we are all capable of great wickedness. In fact, as we know only too well from our society, we are all capable of plumbing the depths of depravity.

In the same way, we are not righteous; we are unrighteous. We do not always do what is right. Given unrestrained choices, most of us would deliberately choose to do wrong. And as far as justice is concerned, although we all want it in society we seldom want justice to apply to us. That is why, for instance, we try so hard to get out of paying traffic fines.

If these things are true then, because God is righteous and must do what is right, the only right thing He can do with us is to condemn us. Salvation therefore means that God had to find a way to accept us and forgive us without in any way violating His own character of holiness and righteousness. And this is exactly what He did. Let us look at this more closely.

RIGHTEOUSNESS

The first concept to grasp is *righteousness*. Take a moment to read Romans 3:21-24:

> But now a righteousness from God, apart from law, has been made known, to which the Law and the Prophets testify. This righteousness from God comes through faith in Jesus Christ to all who believe. There is no difference, for all have sinned and fall short of the glory of God, and are justified freely by his grace through the redemption that came by Christ Jesus.

To be accepted by God we have to be as righteous as He is. Anything less than perfection is unacceptable to Him. To be right in all we do, say or think is simply to be like God. That is the standard requirement to be accepted by God and granted salvation. But, as we know, this is an impossible requirement. We have all sinned. Not one of us is righteous in the sense of being acceptable to God. What are we to do? The answer is that we can do nothing. However, God Himself has done something about it. He provided righteousness for us in His Son, Jesus Christ our Lord. How did He do this?

You will remember that Jesus had no earthly father. He was miraculously conceived in the womb of the Virgin Mary. This aspect of Christ is important. It indicates that He was divine yet human – born of a woman. The only other person created without sin was Adam. As we all know, Adam failed. At the crucial moment he chose his own will over the revealed will of God. Jesus lived for thirty-three years without sinning in thought, word or deed. In other words, He succeeded where Adam failed. That is why He is called 'the last Adam' (1 Cor. 15:45).

God accepted the righteous life Jesus lived and offers Christ's merits to us. When we receive Jesus as our personal Saviour, an amazing transaction takes place. Our unrighteousness, which keeps us from God, is transferred to Jesus. Our sinfulness is viewed as having already been punished when Jesus died on the cross. His perfect life is transferred to our account and viewed by God as belonging to us. God now looks upon us as if we have lived as Jesus did – sinless and perfect in everything.

This is amazing, wonderful and true! No matter how bad you may have been, what harm you may have caused, how unworthy you may feel – when you surrender your life to Christ all your guilt is taken away and you are given a new standing with God that makes you acceptable to Him.

Think for a moment of all you have done that makes you ashamed or causes regret. Do you think you are worthy of forgiveness or acceptance? Of course not! What God has done for us in Jesus is for the unworthy, for people like us. Because we do not deserve it, it is called 'grace'. Grace means not merely undeserved favour and love, but undeserved favour and love to those who deserve the exact opposite. Not only do we have no claim on God's grace, but rather we deserve the exact opposite. We have offended Him and deserve nothing but His judgement. Instead, when we come to Jesus, He not only pardons us but attributes to us a righteousness and personal integrity that we do not deserve and which make us acceptable to Him.

This is true of you! You need to understand this if you want to enjoy assurance. Say to yourself: 'This is true of me. I don't deserve it, but it is true. I am a sinner, undeserving and unable to please God. But He has given *me* the righteousness of Jesus and He has accepted me – even me'.

Does this happen automatically? No! Is it true of all people? No! It is only true of those who put their faith and trust in Jesus Christ. That is why it is 'through faith in Jesus Christ' (Rom. 3:22). The moment you put your faith in Jesus Christ, consciously trusting Him and Him alone for forgiveness of sins and eternal salvation, you are given this righteousness.

Study Questions
Read Romans 3:21-24.

1. Before you became a Christian, what did you think was required to be called 'righteous'? What do you think Paul is referring to by the word 'works' in Ephesians 2:8-9?

2. In what ways do people try to be 'righteous' these days?

3. Read Isaiah 64:6. Why does God take such a dim view of 'our righteous acts'?

4. Read 2 Corinthians 5:21. In what way have we become the righteousness of God in Christ?

5. What response do you think should be drawn from those who have received God's undeserved favour? Are you making that response yourself?

3

Justification

The second important Bible concept to understand is *justification*. It is another way of describing what God has done for us in Christ. Romans 5:1 says:

> Therefore, since we have been justified through faith, we have peace with God through our Lord Jesus Christ.

This word 'Justification' is of immense importance to our sense of inner assurance and wellbeing with God. It means that God, having bestowed a righteousness on us that is acceptable to Him, now declares us to be 'just' human beings. We have been justified against all the accusations of sin and imperfection levelled against us! This does not mean that we are perfect in our daily living. Rather it means that God no longer holds our sins against us.

Isn't this what we need to hear? Isn't this the answer to the problem that troubles Christians? What about my sins and mistakes, my personal failures? The answer is that we have been justified.

This is a Bible doctrine of such importance that we must stay with it for a while. To illustrate it, turn to Romans 4:6-8:

> David says the same thing when he speaks of the blessedness of the man to whom God credits righteousness apart from works: 'Blessed are they whose transgressions are forgiven, whose sins are covered. Blessed is the man whose sin the Lord will never count against him'.

The apostle Paul quotes the first two verses of Psalm 32 to give us a vivid description of what it means to be forgiven, pardoned and justified by God. The first part of verse seven tells us that the truly happy, blessed man is the one whose transgressions – all his wrongdoings – are forgiven. That is well and good. But notice how, in typical Hebrew poetic style, this statement of forgiveness is repeated – 'whose sins are covered'.

I want you to notice the word 'covered'. This word is used in other places in the Old Testament. If we understand how it is used, we will see the impact it can have on our experience of spiritual assurance and certainty.

Firstly it is used in Genesis 9:23 of the action of Shem and Japheth when they 'covered' their father Noah who was lying naked in a drunken stupor. Clearly the Bible means us to understand that something shameful had occurred and Noah's two sons did the right thing in 'covering' him.

The word is used again in Exodus 15:10 after God's miraculous deliverance of the Israelites from the Egyptians through the Red Sea. Moses and Miriam extol God's greatness and power in delivering His people and judging His enemies by singing:

> But you blew with your breath, and the sea covered them.

The Egyptian army was completely covered by the waters and annihilated. Thus we get the idea of how this word is used. It means to cover the shame, enmity and defeat.

There is a third example for us to note. This illustration occurs in Deuteronomy 23:13. It is a daring analogy of what it means to have our sins covered.

> As part of your equipment have something to dig with, and when you relieve yourself, dig a hole and cover up your excrement.

Have you ever wondered how the vast numbers of Israelites, wandering around as nomads in the deserts and wilderness of Sinai for forty years, took care of their toilet arrangements? This verse tells us. How amazing that the great God of the universe should legislate about such a thing! Even in something so mundane, there is a great lesson to be learned. Each Israelite had a digging instrument, probably similar to a small paddle or spade. With this he covered his own excrement so that there would be no disease in the camp.

There is a connection we need to grasp. The same word used to 'cover' human excrement in Deuteronomy 23:13 is the word God uses in Psalm 32:1 to describe what He does with our sins. Can you imagine anything as gross as someone going to such a polluted place and digging up the human waste? Yet this is what we often do in relation to our sins. When God has covered them, we dig them up. We use them to plague us with worry and doubt. No wonder we are robbed of assurance!

Let us turn again to Romans 4:8. Notice what it says about our sins:

> Blessed is the man whose sin the Lord will never count against him.

The Lord will never count it against us. Do you get that? Often our conscience continues to count our sins against us. Sometimes even our friends and families continue to hold our failures against us. But the wonder of the gospel is that when we come to Christ in faith, God takes our sins and covers them.

It is true that sometimes the sins we have committed are a stench to humanity and to God. It may be true that the harm we have done can never be undone in this life. You may feel you are vile, loathsome and hateful. You may even be tempted to think that what you have done is so bad that it has put you beyond the reach of salvation. Think of your sins one by one for a moment. Think of what your actions may have done to others, even to your own family. You may have paid a terrific price in terms of condemnation, alienation and loneliness because of who and what you are.

The great news is that Jesus died for sinners; all who come to Him with genuine repentance and faith have their sins covered. It is almost as if God has used the cross upon which Jesus died as a divine spade and dug a hole so deep that the bottom cannot be seen. Into that hole He has piled the sorry failures of our lives. He has covered them over with load upon load of divine grace. Our sins have been covered and God no longer counts them against us.

Now go back to the first word in Romans 4:7 and in Romans 4:8. The word 'blessed' means to be happy, relieved, contented, to experience a sense of wellbeing. There is hardly a synonym for it. It expresses an inner sense of joy and assurance. Why should you not have this?

David, who penned these words, was a man of blood. He was a murderer and an adulterer. He saw his own family torn asunder by jealousy, lust and treachery. Yet he knew the reality of having his sins covered and he felt blessed. Yes, you can be sure. To be justified means that your sins have been forgiven and forgotten, for ever. God now treats you as if you had never sinned. Somebody has said that 'justified' means 'just-as-if-I-had-never-sinned'.

Take the trouble to read Hebrews 8:7-13 where the writer quotes from Jeremiah 31:31-34. The last words are such a comfort to all spiritual strugglers.

> For I will forgive their wickedness, and will remember their sins no more. (Heb. 8:12 and Jer. 31:34)

Your sins are forgiven and forgotten forever!

All this is true. You do not need to live with doubt and uncertainty. All your sins are really forgiven if you have come to Christ. Dare to believe it. Dare to be happy. Dare to rejoice. You must rejoice! You must be conscious of the joy of forgiveness. That is what the word 'blessed' means. That is what the Bible refers to when it speaks of joy in all its various contexts.

We usually associate joy with happiness. Happiness to us mostly means good and advantageous circumstances. We often take it to mean the absence of those things that could cause strife, tension, hardship or fear. But the Bible associates joy with the consequences of our relationship with God. It is always the joy, the blessedness of knowing that God will never count my sins against me again – not only the sins of the past, but all the sins and failures of the present and the future as well.

Assurance comes from knowing this, from believing that we are loved and accepted. To live your entire Christian life with doubt and uncertainty is to stunt your growth and to spoil your enjoyment of God. This does not, of course, mean that your life will be one of unclouded happiness, or that tough times will not come. Rather it means that no matter how bewildering life may become, the one thing that cannot be taken from you is the fact that you belong to God. That fact is your anchor and hope and it is also the centre of what we call 'joy', not a 'jump up and down' feeling of relief, but a deep awareness that I am in the grip of Someone much bigger than me and He will not let me go.

Don't allow yourself to be spiritually deprived of the assurance of your Father's love. If you have never experienced the blessedness of those whose sins are covered, it will affect every area of your life – your prayers, spiritual understanding, fellowship and zeal. Allow yourself the joy of believing that the Father's arms are around you. You have been justified. You have been given a righteousness that makes you acceptable to Him. You do not deserve it. You cannot earn it. But it is yours. You are blessed. Dare to believe it and enjoy it.

Study Questions

Read Romans 4:6-8.

1. Read pages 25-31 again.

    - Do you think that some of your sins are so bad that God either will not or cannot 'cover' them?

    - Do you believe that your sins are 'covered'?

    Read Psalm 103:3, Micah 7:18-19.

2. If God justifies us and 'covers' our sins, do we have any right to keep dwelling upon them?

    Read Romans 8:33-34.

3. Do you believe God loves you...

    - because you are lovable?

    - because you are kind-hearted by nature?

    - because you have lived a good life?

    - because of His grace?

4. Read Deuteronomy 7:7-8.

    - Does this apply to us today?

    - How?

    - Are you sure He loves you?

5. Read John 17:23.

    - What do you think it means?

4

More about justification

We must stay with the teaching of justification for a while longer. There is so much for us to understand and the more we understand, the greater the assurance we will enjoy.

Justification is, in fact, God making a declaration about us. To be justified means to be acquitted. It is a legal act. It is God saying 'according to my law, you are no longer blameworthy. Rather, I now regard you as blameless'.

It is important for us to put this great teaching into perspective. To be declared blameless does not mean that we are righteous in the sense that we no longer actually commit sin. Rather it means that God regards us as being righteous and legally declares us to be so. We may still be conscious of sin and we may still actually commit sin, but from a legal point of view we are blameless.

Imagine that at this moment you are in a great courtroom somewhere in eternity. Picture the scene. The great Judge of all the earth is at the bar and the record books are open before Him. You stand in the dock ashamed and fearful. You are about to answer for all the deeds done in the flesh. Three witnesses have come to testify against you, the Bible, the devil and your conscience.

The great Judge calls the first witness. The Bible steps forward and informs Him that you ought to be found guilty. 'O Judge,' says the Bible, 'this person has not kept your laws, choosing his own way. He must be found guilty.'

You hang your head in shame. You know it is all true. You think of the occasions when you had the opportunity to hear the Bible being taught. You remember the times you spurned the overtures of Christian friends and laughed at those who were believers. You are guilty.

The Judge calls the second witness. The devil, the great enemy of your soul, steps forward.

'O Judge,' he says, 'this man must be condemned because he fell for every temptation I set for him. He was careless and negligent. He never watched his step and time after time he committed sin against you. He was blind. He could not see me at work. In his ignorance, he was easy to delude. He must be condemned.'

Your shoulders slump even more. It's all true. Your mind races back over the years. You remember how, with careless abandon, you did exactly what you wanted to do. You thought you could get away with it. Sometimes you didn't even care if you were found out. People were hurt in the process. Your great concern was to gratify your desires. You fell into temptation. You are guilty.

Now the third witness steps up to the witness box. It's your conscience.

'O Judge,' your conscience says, 'this man deliberately flouted every warning I gave him, every nudge, and every restraint. He deliberately blunted my pleadings and snuffed out my voice. Time after time I tried to remind him of lessons he had heard as a child in Sunday school and things his parents had taught him, but he was so obsessed with himself and his own desires that he thrust me aside until I could stir him no longer. He is guilty of silencing my voice and going his own way. He must be punished.'

How ashamed you feel! You remember with overwhelming guilt the times you did things you knew were wrong. The strange power of sin took hold of your heart and carried you away. Your lusts, prejudices and unbelief took you in a direction which you knew to be quite wrong. But year after year you followed the impulses of your heart. You thought you were free, but you were not free at all. You were a prisoner of prisoners. You were in chains, dragged off by blindness and desire. Now you stand before God and you are guilty.

A hush falls over the courtroom. The witnesses have given their evidence. The Judge must pass sentence. He calls you.

'All that these three witnesses have said is true. My judgement is that the soul that sins must die. I therefore sentence you to eternal death, there to bear my wrath from everlasting to everlasting.'

An awful solemnity pervades the courtroom. You have nothing to say. What can you say? It's all true. You are guilty. All your life you ignored the Bible. You thought you were too clever for God's book, or that there would be time enough for it later. All your life you followed the inclinations and desires of your heart. You did just as you pleased, with no regard for who got hurt or what was right or wrong. You were the devil's own fool. All your life you managed to shove those twinges of conscience to the back of your mind, until the dim echo of its voice was finally lost. Now you stand condemned.

But wait! Who is this stepping out from the crowd? Why! It is Jesus. He comes to act as your Advocate. Note how He addresses the Judge – He walks up to the bar and looks into the great and terrifying eyes of this Person who sees all things, including your heart.

'Father, wait,' He says.

The Judge pauses. And as He looks at His Son Jesus, your Advocate, the terrible and beautiful face of the Judge takes on a peculiar tenderness.

'I do not come to plead the innocence of this person,' Jesus says. 'He is guilty. I have no defence to offer on his behalf, except this.' He holds up His hands and the judge sees the imprint of the nails.

The great eternal punishment placed on your shoulders has already been paid on the cross by your Advocate. There your sentence was carried out. Every stroke has been accounted for. He died for you. It was your punishment He bore.

As the Judge sees the nail prints in the hands of His Son, He takes up His pen and writes 'cancelled' across your charge sheet. Your debt has been paid. Punishment has been meted out. Justice has been done. The Judge takes off His gown and dons the robe of a father. He takes you by one arm and His Son takes you by the other. And in the tenderest way possible, they walk you out of the courtroom and into the sunshine, never to be judged again. You have been acquitted. You will never appear in that courtroom again.

Having your sins forgiven is the greatest event in the entire world. No wonder Paul writes these amazing words:

> Therefore, there is now no condemnation for those who are in Christ Jesus, because through Christ Jesus the law of the Spirit of life set me free from the law of sin and death. (Rom. 8:1-2)

No condemnation. What a statement! Millions live their lives under the condemnation of God who, although loving, is also holy and just. But the man or woman who comes to Christ has been, in a figurative sense, into the courtroom of divine justice and there, by virtue of Christ's death on the cross, has been acquitted. This means that sin can never again be held against you in the same way as it can for an unbeliever. You have been redeemed by the precious blood of Jesus Christ. Not with silver or gold, but with His blood and by His death. And, because of who He is, that atonement stands for ever. The punishment has been borne.

Your conscience may not always allow you to feel forgiven. Although the conscience is a gift from God, it can be a great problem by insisting that we are still guilty. The devil certainly won't take this acquittal of yours lying down. He will roar against you and redouble his temptations. As you read the Bible, you may become aware of how uncompromising the law of God is. Its severity may strike to your heart. Be that as it may, you are no longer condemned. You are free.

Lucky Malaza was a criminal in South Africa who through an administrative error was granted amnesty and freed. When the mistake was discovered there was a national furore. Various options were looked at to see if he could be rearrested. The debate raged loud and long. But at the end of the day he remained a free man because of the amnesty. The state had declared him free and free he was. He could no longer be brought to court for any of his past crimes. As far as the law was concerned his crimes were dealt with for good. The difference was, of course, that he was freed from paying for his crimes whereas we are freed precisely because our sin was paid for by Christ. But his story does illustrate the truth that the law was unable to touch him after he had been 'forgiven'.

That is the way it is between Christians and God. We have been acquitted. We are no longer in the courtroom. Though we have been guilty of sin in the past, now our crimes have been paid for. Our punishment has been cancelled and we are indeed free.

There is however a great difference between Lucky Malaza and us. Malaza was freed only of the past crimes, not of any future misdemeanours. In fact, he did run foul of the law again and was rearrested and finally imprisoned. But for the believer, justification means pardon not only for the past but for the present and the future as well.

This may constitute a problem for some people. Does this mean that, regardless of what we do, it no longer matters? Does it mean that we will be saved no matter what? We must be careful not to go further than the Bible does. We must remember that this great act of justification includes the gift of a new nature. This new nature has new desires and new aspirations. This new nature seeks to reflect Jesus in all things.

People who claim to be justified or pardoned yet continue to live as they please may use the right words or expressions, but they do not have the right experience. When God justifies us, He also gives us a new nature that will love Him and seek to please Him in the way we live.

Therefore, to be justified is to be caught up in such a wondrous act of grace that we can never be the same again. We may stumble, slip and fall. We may do many things that make us ashamed, but we cannot be the same as we were before and we cannot be brought into the courtroom again. We have been acquitted. Our sins have been forgiven and forgotten for ever. To live as unbelievers do is simply to prove that we have never been justified.

JUSTIFICATION IS FREE

There is still more to consider on this subject. Look again at Romans 3:24:

... justified freely by his grace through the redemption that came by Christ Jesus.

We must grasp this concept of being 'justified freely
by his grace'. I have met many Christians who have
often heard this phrase but have never enjoyed real
spiritual assurance because, strangely, they have
somehow never appropriated these words for themselves. The truth of these words remains outside the
realm of their daily experience.

Do not be impatient with me if I reiterate that
our acceptance by God, the gift of righteousness
that He gives us, the great declaration that we are
acquitted, does not depend on how good we are
or on how good we are trying to be. Many sincere
Christians truly turn to Christ in faith and then attempt to live their daily lives in an effort to be so
good that God will not be displeased with them.
While it is right to try to please God in our daily life, if the element of faith is lost and the joy of
serving Him becomes a series of legalistic duties to
merit His approval, we have missed the point. We
are like the Christians in Galatia who began in the
Spirit but continued by human effort (Gal. 3:3).

Our sense of assurance has nothing whatever to do
with seeking to be holy in a legalistic or perfectionistic
sense. Acceptance by God and the enjoyment of His
favour has nothing to do with our deeds. We must get
this right. I am not suggesting that deeds and lifestyles

do not matter. They do matter. If we allow sin to settle in our lives, we grieve the Holy Spirit and lose the sense of His presence. But God accepts us even if we are not perfect because all our imperfections have been paid for by Christ.

We must learn to transfer our dependence from our miserable attempts at being good to Christ's all-sufficient payment for us on the cross. Some Christians may sincerely think that they trust Christ and not their own efforts, yet they often feel miserable and alienated from God. If you feel this way, test yourself with these questions:

- Do you feel that you have failed spiritually if you miss your daily personal devotions or fail to attend church one Sunday morning?

- Do you feel alienated from God if you are unable to cope with the fatigue of daily work plus running a home?

- If you get depressed, do you feel guilty? Do you feel that you should always be happy and victorious? If you aren't feeling that way, do you pretend you are or do you simply feel bad?

If you answered yes to these three questions, you have given yourself away. You are trusting in your daily performance rather than in God's great pardon which has freed you forever.

We should be doing the best we can, with God's help, to live a life that is pleasing to Him. But we should not trust or depend on our own efforts for acceptance with God or the sense of His blessing and approval. For that inner sense of His love, we do not look to our efforts but rather in faith trust His promise to accept us and love us.

Look at it this way. You will never deserve God's blessing even if you spend five hours in prayer daily. There is nothing, absolutely nothing you can do to deserve to be justified 'freely by his grace' (Rom. 3:24).

GRACE

'*Grace*' is a wonderful New Testament word in which all Christians believe, but not all rely on it. It means unmerited favour or kindness shown to the utterly undeserving. In fact, grace refers to the kindness of God shown to those who deserve the exact opposite. It is not as if we were merely neutral and ignorant while we were unsaved. We were positively at enmity with God (Rom. 5:8).

Yet His grace is extended to us in our enmity – to us, people who would otherwise have no hope.

Does this mean that our daily deeds do not matter? Does it mean that attempts to grow and make progress in the Christian life have no value? On the contrary, our deeds are most important. But that discussion must wait a while because we have not finished with justification.

JUSTIFICATION IS COSTLY

Come back with me to Romans 3:24. Notice the words, 'the redemption that came by Christ Jesus'. Did I say that our salvation was free? Yes – to us. But it was not free to Christ. It cost Him His life! Go back for a moment to the courtroom scene. See the Saviour, your Advocate, hold up His hands. See the nail prints there. What pain and suffering did it cost for us to be acquitted? Our justification went beyond pain and suffering; it went as far as death. The Son of God gave Himself for my sins.

Notice the word 'redemption' in this verse. It dates back to the slave markets of old when slaves were put on stands, shackled, helpless and miserable, to be purchased by anyone who fancied them. They became the property of their new owner to do with as he pleased. He could treat them kindly or cruelly. He could kill them if he wished. They were his property.

Imagine a buyer coming to the market and you are the slave on the stand. You are far away from home, alone, friendless and afraid. You do not know what the future holds. You are caught in depression and despair. The buyer stands before you and says to the dealer, 'I'll take him.' The price is agreed. 'Unlock his shackles,' says the buyer. It is done; the deal is concluded. You kneel mutely before your new owner. What will he say to you, do to you or expect of you? Then come the words, 'I have paid the price to redeem you. You are mine to do as I please. I therefore release you. You are a free man to come and go as you please. You will never be a slave again. Here are your redemption papers.' You are surprised and stunned. Your heart is filled with relief and gratitude. You say to your benefactor, 'Such a master I will serve freely, willingly and gladly all my life.' This is what Jesus did for you. But what was the redemption price? Look at Romans 3:25:

> God presented him as a sacrifice of atonement, through faith in his blood. He did this to demonstrate his justice, because in his forbearance he had left the sins committed beforehand unpunished ...

Notice the part Jesus played in our redemption. He was a sacrifice. It is faith in His blood that saves us. The redemption price was His own blood.

But look more closely at this incredible truth. God presented Him as a sacrifice. His own Father did this. Here is love such as the world has never seen and would never understand were it not for God's grace that opens our blind eyes.

This verse takes us back to that great chapter, Isaiah 53. Notice the phrase used in verses four to six to describe what happened on the cross:

- stricken by God

- smitten by Him and afflicted

- pierced for our transgressions

- crushed for our iniquities

- the Lord has laid on Him the iniquity of us all

Let us be very careful before we doubt God's love for us. The most amazing language is used to describe the price God paid for our redemption. Let us also acknowledge our utter inability to understand the great mystery of God giving up His Son. What did it cost God? How did God feel? Who can tell? Who can plumb these mysteries? What did it cost Jesus to be crushed by His own Father? What great and profound mysteries are locked in the words of Romans 3:25?

'God presented him as a sacrifice of atonement ...'

This act is underscored in an even more graphic way in Galatians 3:1:

You foolish Galatians! Who has bewitched you? Before your very eyes Jesus Christ was clearly portrayed as crucified.

The word 'portrayed' means to be 'placarded' like a protester's banner or an advertisement. This is how Jesus was preached to the Galatians. What was it that Paul thought fit to placard before the Galatians? Christ's birth? No! His life and miracles? No! His matchless teachings? No! Rather it was His crucifixion. That is the heart of the gospel. The cost, the price of our justification, was His own blood.

For us to have assurance we must believe, not merely in the fact of His suffering on the cross, but also that it was for us. He was our substitute. Here is another word for your 'assurance vocabulary' – *substitutionary*. It means that all the wrath Jesus endured on the cross as He atoned for our sins was for us. He was our substitute. Our justification was costly indeed.

Somebody has pointed out that there are four ideas contained in the word 'sacrifice' as it is used in the Bible. Firstly, it refers to an *offence* that has to be taken away. That offence is our sin and rebellion. To be accepted by God, the question of our guilt has to be dealt with. Secondly, the word implies that there is a *person* who needs to be pacified by the sacrifice that is offered. Of course, we know that there is such a person – God Himself – who is constantly offended by our sinfulness and rebellion. The third implication is that there is an *offender*. Here the reference is not merely to the offence but also to the perpetrator of the offence. That's us. We are the guilty ones. Fourthly, sacrifice implies that there is a *means* of making atonement and appeasing the offended one. The sacrifice has to be sufficient in magnitude to cover the offence and placate the injured party. That is exactly what the sacrifice of Jesus was – sufficient to meet the standards and requirements of a Holy God, sufficient to atone for the worst of sin and the worst of sinners.

We must be careful that, in thinking about God and sacrifice in this way, we do not see Him as a primitive deity who is unpredictable and capricious by nature. He is not a mythological character who is nice to people one moment and filled with a hostility that needs to be appeased by sacrifice the next. Rather, we are dealing with the fact that God is holy and just. His attitude towards sin is consistent – He opposes it and judges it. But there was no atonement we could make that would be acceptable to God.

When we put our trust in Christ, God's wrath is satisfied. Jesus' blood is enough. Nothing else is required. The value of Jesus' blood lies in the fact that it was innocent – free from all sin. Our guilt is transferred to Him, His innocence to us. We are free. The cost, great as it was, was sufficient. We are gladly, warmly, graciously accepted by God. Our sins are forgiven and forgotten forever.

But wait! That is not all. There is an element to Jesus' death on the cross that we must always bear in mind. In Romans 3:25-26 one word occurs twice. It is the word 'justice'. Why this method of atonement?

Why the blood of atonement? Because God is righteous and must judge sin. God must be a God who judges or else nothing makes sense any more.

We must remember that the death of Jesus on the cross did not change God's mind about anything. Jesus carried out the will of God that existed from the beginning of time. He did not merely die on the cross; He experienced the wrath of God that led to death. This was part of God's plan before the world was created (Eph. 1:4) so that we may be saved and *know the blessedness of it.*

Our joy comes from knowing that, although we keep on falling, the blood of Jesus keeps on cleansing us. Our title deeds to glory have been signed and sealed by blood – Jesus' blood. Our salvation can never be undone. We can be sure of that.

Think of it in this way. Everything you ever were, everything you are and everything you will ever be or do is under the blood of Christ. All has been paid for. God has pronounced you righteous. If you have repented of your sins and truly trusted Christ and Christ alone, *you will go to heaven.* In the words of the old hymn:

There is a fountain filled with blood
Drawn from Emmanuel's veins;
And sinners plunged beneath that flood
Lose all their guilty stains.
(William Cowper)

Christians talk about the 'blood of Jesus' and His 'death' on a cross. Why? It is a way of saying that the penalty for our sin has been paid. There has to be a payment as atonement for us to be free. I have a newspaper cartoon in my files that appeared one Easter. It depicts three crosses on a hill with the city of Jerusalem in the background. Three forlorn-looking men are walking down the hill. The caption reads: 'What I cannot understand is why he had to go through all the agony to forgive our sins when he could have just forgotten them.' Therein lies the mystery for those who do not understand. God could not just have forgotten them, nor could He simply forgive them. Sin had to be accounted for or else God would not be just. There had to be atonement. Jesus provided that atonement. Now your sins are forgiven and forgotten, *forever*.

Study Questions

Read Romans 3:21-26.

1. Write out in three or four simple sentences what you think the Bible means by 'justification'.

2. If you have been justified by God, do you think you can ever again face the prospect of eternal damnation? Why not?

   Read Romans 8:33-34.

3. Read Romans 3:24.

    • Was your salvation really free?

    • Who paid the price? (read p. 44)

4. If you are feeling unsure of yourself spiritually, which of the three options should you be concentrating on?

    • Trying harder?

    • More prayer?

    • Faith in what Christ has already done?

5. What do the following words mean?

    • Grace (p. 43)

    • Redemption (p. 44)

    • Substitutionary (p. 47)

6. Discuss the four elements in the biblical idea of sacrifice (pp. 47-48).

5

Peace with God

We turn to Romans 5:1:

> 'Therefore, since we have been justified through
> faith, we have peace with God through our Lord
> Jesus Christ ...'

Once we have been justified by faith in Christ
a number of blessings follow. At least three blessings
are mentioned in the opening verses of Romans 5
that are very important to our personal assurance.
These are peace with God, access into the realm of
grace and blessing and the hope of the glory of God.
Because we are justified, our ultimate and complete
salvation is certain, guaranteed and absolute. But
with that certainty come certain privileges which
belong to us. Sadly, many Christians fail to grasp
this.

In his great commentaries on Romans,[1] Dr Martyn Lloyd-Jones pauses to draw attention to the phrase 'through our Lord Jesus Christ'. He reminds us that Christ's Name is constantly set before us because He is the means of every blessing. Nothing would be ours – no forgiveness, no hope and no blessing – were it not for His death and resurrection. We receive everything through Him and nothing without Him. Christ is all to us.

Having underscored that, let us look at the first and most important blessing that flows from God's gracious act of justifying us.

PEACE WITH GOD

When we think of the things we would like God to give us, many people put other things first. Some would choose happiness, an absence of trouble or strife, a knowledge that all our circumstances are in order. Some who may be struggling with a serious illness, or have a loved one who is sick, would want healing of the body and freedom from disease. Often such people see healing or health as the greatest possible blessing. Yet others can conceive of no greater blessing than to have all their material needs met. Provision to pay debts and obtain all we need for bodily comfort is the epitome of blessing for some.

---

1   Lloyd-Jones, Martyn, *Romans*, Edinburgh, Banner of Truth, 1971.

The problem is that all too often we lose our sense of assurance because we interpret our circumstances wrongly. We assume that, if our circumstances are difficult or if ill health or poverty comes upon us, something is wrong with us spiritually. We lose our sense of His love and sink into despair or confusion. But this is wrong. None of these things describe what the Bible means when it talks of 'peace with God'. Let us do away once and for all with all these wrong notions of what it means to have peace with God.

Firstly, it does not refer to peace in a general sense. Peace with God has nothing to do with a vague inner sense of tranquillity. Many people who are not Christians enjoy that. For some people the feeling is induced by medication or narcotics. The peace we need is far more urgent than that. We are in a state of war with God. What we need is a state where all hostilities between us and God cease. The peace we need is not merely rooted in the emotions but in the human spirit and in the conscience.

Secondly, we must make it clear that this peace does not refer to the peace *of* God, i.e. the sense of wellbeing that issues from God. That is an entirely different kind of peace and is mentioned in Philippians 4:7. It pertains to a completely different situation. We do need God's peace when we are surrounded by problems, when circumstances seem out of control, when ill health strikes or when needs arise that exhaust all human resources. Thousands of Christians can testify to 'the peace of God, which transcends all understanding' possessing them at such times. But this is not what is meant by peace *with* God and it is not our primary need in relation to our sense of assurance. One deals with sin and the other with circumstances.

What then does this phrase 'peace with God' mean? Why is it the foremost blessing arising out of justification? The simple answer is that the first thing we need is a way back to God. The gospel's primary function is to bring us back to God. There can be no other blessing until we are reconciled to God. Thus the most important result of justification by faith is peace with God.

Peace with God is available to us only because Christ has turned away the wrath of God. Sin has been dealt with. Christ's atonement does not merely declare a truce between us and God; it reconciles God to us in an everlasting covenant which can never be broken. God will never be at war with us again.

Is this important? If you struggle with being sure of God's acceptance, ask yourself why that is. Usually it is because you have a niggling fear that something you are doing is not quite right. Many people feel that they do not have enough faith or, for that matter, the right kind of faith. The consequences are that they live for years with the feeling – undefined and difficult to articulate – that God is not entirely pleased with them. They fear that they have offended Him. They despair of ever being holy enough for Him.

The first great consequence of turning to Christ and being justified by faith is peace with God – you need never again fear the displeasure of God. You are accepted in Christ. He loves you and includes you in His great covenant of grace. You must now consciously face your fears and measure them against the truth contained in Romans 5:1:

> Therefore, since we have been justified through faith, we have peace with God through our Lord Jesus Christ.

Peace with God is not something we strive for. It is something we now have, by faith in Christ. Read again the words in Romans 3:24: '... and are justified.' This is present tense. It is a present reality. It is not something that will happen to us on a future day of judgement if we live correctly and keep the laws. No! It is ours now. Now and present, we are declared to be in the right with God. True, we don't deserve it. True, we could not of ourselves believe it. But God has brought us to trust in Christ, and if He has done that, we have been justified. The state of enmity between us and God has ceased.

We should stop our spiritual cowering. God is not about to strike us at any moment. He is now our Father. Our status has changed. Our relationship with Him has changed. We may not at this moment enjoy too much of the peace of God. Yet that does not rule out the great truth that when we put our faith in Jesus Christ we receive *peace with God,* through faith. 'Ah yes faith', I can hear someone say, 'that's my problem. I just can't seem to believe properly. I don't have enough faith.' Well let's discuss that!

Study Questions

Read Romans 5:1-3.

1. What does it mean to have peace with God?

2. What role does Christ play in giving me peace with God? Compare Romans 1:1-7 (concentrate on v. 7) with Romans 5:1-3.

3. Read Romans 5:1 and Philippians 4:7.

   What is the difference between peace *with* God and the peace *of* God? (p. 55)

4. What sort of struggle must you undertake to obtain peace with God? (p. 56)

5. Is peace with God really possible in this life? If so, do you enjoy it?

6. If you don't enjoy peace with God, can you think of a reason for this?

6

Faith

Everything we receive from God is by faith in Jesus Christ. The matter of exercising faith is a profound problem for many people. They don't know how to do it or what to expect when they do. So let's ask the question: 'What is faith?' Let us look at three statements about faith by way of definition, then I want to ask you a few questions to help you establish whether you have faith or not.

TRUST

The first and simplest thing to say about faith is that it is *trust*. It is simply believing that God will, in fact, do what He promises. A famous Old Testament illustration of this is the story of Abraham (Gen. 12:1-4, 15:3-6).

The substance of this story is that God promised Abraham something which was humanly impossible at that stage in his life – a son. Yet, impossible though it may have been from a physical and bio-logical point of view, Genesis 15:6 records:

> Abram believed the Lord, and he credited it to
> him as righteousness.

What does it mean when it says that 'Abram believed the Lord'? It is no different to what you are asked to do when you are invited to believe Jesus. Simply believe that God does not tell lies! What He says, He will do. He will always keep His word. Not one of His promises to us will be broken.

Now read Romans 4:18-25. Here we discover an affirmation of what happened to Abraham – his trust in God was credited to him as righteousness. This was written for our benefit to illustrate the way God credits us with righteousness if we trust Him or put our faith in Him.

I know that many Christians struggle with the question of assurance because they do not grasp the concept of faith. Let me illustrate faith further by using a very familiar analogy – that of marriage. When two people make marriage vows to each other, what are they actually doing? Think about it. They trust each other with themselves. It is an act of faith. You honestly believe that your partner will keep the vows made on your wedding day and that, emotionally and physically, you will be loved and cared for until death parts you.

We know only too well that this analogy breaks down because of the fallenness of human nature. Many people do not keep their vows and often untold hurt and damage is caused. But at the outset it is a matter of trust.

So it is when you come to Christ. You trust Him. The difference is that He never breaks His promise. He cannot because He is holy and righteous. When God declares you righteous because you trusted Jesus, it is forever. You need not be cautious, diffident, scared or nervous. He really accepts you for ever. But you must *trust* Him. Believe that He does not tell lies. He does and will accept you. But what if He doesn't? You may ask. If He doesn't, it's the end of the line for us. Then there is no gospel and if there is a God, He is proved to be evil, for He has misled us all. No dear friend, no such possibilities exist. God is good. There is no evil in Him, He will never turn you away (John 6:37). But when you come, you must abandon yourself to Him, trust Him, let go of your doubts. Do not use your attempts at being good as a sort of plan B. Rather it is to be a conscious act of *trusting God to be true to His word.*

A RELATIONSHIP

Secondly, faith implies a *relationship*. Notice what it says in Romans 4:3 'Abraham believed God.' God is a person – not an idea. Abraham's trust was not in an idea or an impersonal philosophy. Many people today trust in intangible things like 'positive thinking' or in New Age philosophies, vague ideas, vibes or influences. But Abraham trusted *God*. So do we. This means that there is a relationship with Him.

You see, it is not the mere act of believing that counts. You have probably heard people who have very little to do with religion say something like, 'I believe that it will all work out'. They have faith in what? Some intangible force? It's almost as if the psychological act of believing has merit in itself. This may have certain psychological benefits in the physical realm, but in the spiritual realm it is worse than useless.

It is not the activity of believing, but the One in whom you believe that is of paramount importance. Imagine how ridiculous it would be for a marriage to take place with only one partner. This partner utters all the vows – to nobody. It is absurd. So too it is ridiculous to think of faith without God as a person receiving that faith and rewarding it.

Faith is a simple act of trust in a person who is infinitely good, who cannot lie and who will keep all His promises. Remember our justification or acceptance by God is by simply trusting His Word that all who come to Jesus will be saved. Have you done that? Then stop worrying about His love for you!

A DIVINE GIFT

But there is a third element to faith for us to remember and it is this. Faith is a *divine gift* from God. In other words, the very ability to trust the Lord Jesus Christ for our salvation is given to us by God in His great love and grace.

God cannot justify us unless we come to Christ. Yet if we are left to our own devices, we will never come to Christ. Men love darkness rather than light (John 3:19). If we naturally gravitate towards the darkness and not the light, how are we ever going to come to Christ to be justified?

The answer is that God Himself breaks through the stubborn resistance of our hearts and gives us the will, the strength and the ability to come to Christ so that He can justify us. Jesus said: 'No one can come to me unless the Father who sent me draws him' (John 6:44). And that is exactly what God has done to you, if you are a believer in Jesus Christ. Is that not wonderful grace? It is something beyond our understanding that God should love us so much. Yet this is the true teaching of scripture. Here are some Bible verses that underline the truth of this assertion.

Yet to all who received him, to those who believed in his name, he gave the right to become children of God – children born not of natural descent, nor of human decision or a husband's will, but born of God. (John 1:12-13)

Then he opened their minds so they could understand the Scriptures' (Luke 24:45).

'For it has been granted to you on behalf of Christ not only to believe on him, but also to suffer for him …. (Phil. 1:29)

For it is by grace you have been saved, through faith – and this not from yourselves, it is the gift of God …. (Eph. 2:8)

One of those listening was a woman named Lydia, a dealer in purple cloth from the city of Thyatira, who was a worshipper of God. The Lord opened her heart to respond to Paul's message. (Acts 16:14)

When the Gentiles heard this, they were glad and honoured the word of the Lord, and all who were appointed for eternal life believed. (Acts 13:48)

We see that our justification is something that happens once for all. It can never be revoked. It is something that happens to all those who have faith in Jesus Christ. This faith is simple trust in God to keep His Word. It is trust in God, not in ourselves and our good works or good ideas. Moreover, this faith is a gift from God so that we can actually come to Christ and be justified.

I know that many Christians are anxious to know that the faith they exercise in Jesus is a real, trusting and saving faith. Many doubt whether they have such faith. How do you know you possess true faith? Is there any way I can test myself? I want to suggest that there is. Let me help you with six simple tests.

SIX TESTS OF TRUE FAITH

Bear in mind that these six tests are merely guidelines. If you can answer 'yes' to them, even if your yes is hesitant, it is fairly certain that you are one of those whose faith is a real saving faith.

1. **Do you believe that Jesus Christ died on the Cross for our sins and that there is no other way of salvation?**

In other words, you can say that you understand salvation through Christ and Christ alone. You have grasped what it means to be justified. This does not necessarily mean that you grasp all the implications or immensity of salvation. You may experience a fluctuation in your feelings about it. But at the bottom of all your inner tumult, you do in fact understand how it is possible that God can forgive you. Do you have that? If you do, it's a good sign.

2. **Do you believe that God has demonstrated His love for you by giving up His Son to the cross, even though you are a sinner and in spite of your sins?**

This is a difficult one and you need to think about it carefully. You may have an enormous sense of your own unworthiness. In fact, you may have been guilty of things that make it difficult for you to understand how God can possibly love you. The problem with many of us is that our past actions or lifestyles make us feel so miserable and unworthy that we don't like ourselves very much. Our self-loathing is often transferred to God. We believe that He loathes us as much as we loathe ourselves.

But having pointed that out, let me put it to you again. In spite of how you may feel about yourself and your own personal unworthiness, though you don't know how or why, do you nevertheless have a deep inner conviction that God loves you in spite of your personal unworthiness? That's also a good sign.

3. **Are you able to handle your own conscience?**

Why do I ask this? Conscience is probably the greatest problem people have as they battle to gain assurance. Do you remember the illustration of the courtroom? Can you recall I said then that conscience will not easily leave you alone? What a powerful force conscience is. Our minds have the power of recall, and many deeds we have committed in the past are placed right at the 'reply' button of our minds. Even though we ask for forgiveness, we are often unsure that it has been granted and so we live with regrets that plague us.

The Christian who has real saving faith will be able to deal with his conscience even though he may not do so perfectly. There may be many a struggle, but the truly justified person will eventually fall back on God's free act of grace in forgiving us.

Conscience often raises questions about our standing with God. Regrets are not easily dealt with. But we must draw a distinction between regrets and guilt. Regrets you may have, but a truly justified person will bring his constant rising feelings of guilt to the cross and remember that Christ has died for Him. We have been washed in His blood and justified by His great grace. We fall back on this again and again because it is the only real basis of hope.

4. Do you refuse to give up in spite of the harassment of Satan?

He will not leave you alone either. He will harass you and accuse you because he is the accuser of Christians (Rev 12:10).

Larry Christenson, a well-known Christian writer, has written a helpful little tract entitled *The Old Landlord*. Here is a section of what he says:

Think of yourselves as living in a block of flats. You have lived there under a landlord who has made your life miserable. He charged you exorbitant rent and when you couldn't pay he loaned you the money at a fearful rate of interest, to get you further in his debt.

He came barging into your apartment at all hours of the day and night, wrecked and dirtied the place up and then charged you extra for not maintaining the premises. Your life was a misery.

Then came someone who said, 'I've taken over this block of flats. I've purchased it and you can live here as long as you like, free. The rent is paid up. I am going to be living here with you in the manager's flat.'

What joy! You are saved! You are delivered out of the clutches of that old landlord! But what happens? You have hardly had the time to rejoice in your new found freedom when a knock comes at the door. And there he is – the old landlord: mean, glowering and demanding as ever. He has come for the rent, he says. What do you do? Do you pay him? Of course you don't! Do you go out and bop him on the nose? No – he's bigger than you!

SATAN DIVERTED

You quietly and confidently tell him, 'You'll have to take it up with the new manager.' He may bellow and threaten, may wheedle and cajole, but you quietly tell him, 'Take it up with the new manager.' And if he comes back a dozen times, with all sorts of threats and arguments, waving all sorts of legal looking papers in your face, you quietly tell him, 'Take it up with the new manager.'

And you know he *has* to, he knows he has to also. He simply hopes that he can bluff and threaten and deceive you into doubting that the new manager will really take care of things.

Now this is the situation of a Christian. Once Christ has delivered you from the power of sin and the devil you can rest assured the old landlord will soon come knocking at the door. And what is your defence? How do you keep him from getting the whip hand over you again? You send him to Jesus.

Do you see what Larry Christenson is saying? The true Christian is no longer accountable to anyone but Christ. When the enemy brings all our old sins against us, we simply refer him to our new landlord – the One who now indwells us. If you are able to do this, however imperfectly, you are on the right track.

5. True saving faith no longer fears death

Left unqualified, this statement will probably cause a great deal of consternation among sincere and sensitive Christians. Few among us do not fear death. In fact, while most of us do fear death, there are certain individuals who seem to have no fear of dying even though they are not Christians. One often discovers acts of great courage in the face of death, especially during times of war. I myself have often been at the bedside of dying people who seem to have little concern about death although they would not claim to be Christians. So what does this statement mean?

Firstly, it does not mean that Christians do not have fears about dying. There is a natural aversion to passing from this life into the next. Even Christians are not exempt from the fears and feelings of concern about loved ones left behind – husbands, wives or small children.

Christians are also not exempt from the trauma that may ensue if they face the prospect of an early death. What about unfinished tasks? Why me? Often we are made to feel that the prospect of an early death is a punishment from God for some sin we have committed. The problem is that we often don't know what that sin is, so we cry, 'Why me? What have I done?' It is possible that in the stress of the process of dying, we may forget that we are not exempt from the sadness and tragedy of living in a fallen and broken world.

Secondly, we must remember that during times of illness, when we are naturally weak, the enemy launches his worst assaults against us. He uses the arrow of doubts to pierce our souls. Thus we are often assailed by doubts about God's love, plans and purposes. We are filled with doubt about our own standing in God's sight. Are we really Christians? Are we truly forgiven and justified?

In his famous classic *The Pilgrim's Progress,* John Bunyan pictures Christian passing through the river of death. As he enters the river, Christian begins to sink and cries out to his friend Hopeful:

> The billows go over my head, all the waves go over me, the sorrows of death have compassed me about ... . And with that a great darkness and horror fell upon Christian.[1]

Needless to say, all turns out well and both Christian and Hopeful make it safely through this profound experience we call death. The point is that, even for Christians, it can be a trying experience made worse by the attacks of the tempter.

But the third fact concerning the Christian and death is that often the problem lies not so much in death itself but rather in the *process* of dying. Often this causes consternation. Christians know what lies beyond – not with arrogant dogmatism, but rather with humble confidence in the reality of God's

---

1   Bunyan, John, *Pilgrim's Progress*, Fearn, Scotland, Christian Focus, 1995.

Word. They know that there is a dimension of glory and happiness that defies human description. But the act of dying can be traumatic, painful and confusing even for those who have been truly justified.

But there is an all-important fourth element that must be considered which puts this into perspective. When we say that the Christian does not fear death, what we mean is that the Christian does not fear death *in the same way* as the unbeliever. The sting of death has been removed for the Christian. Judgement is no longer part of his future. The unbeliever has no such hope. Whatever struggles or fears the Christian may need to endure as he faces the profound experience of dying, he does not fear death in the same way as the unbeliever does. Our judgement is past. It occurred on the cross of Calvary when Jesus made atonement for us. When we placed our trust in Him, that judgement was attributed to Him. We no longer have to face the judgement of sin in the same way as the non-Christian does.

Test yourself in this way. Do you know deep down in your heart, in spite of the uncertainties and the unknown, that death for you will be a doorway into the presence of God?

The last test of faith to consider is one that has given rise to a great deal of misunderstanding in the past. I hope it does not do so for you.

6. A true Christian has confidence in his salvation even when he falls into sin.

I know that this may be surprising for some people, but how can there be assurance for any of us if the sacrifice of Jesus only atoned for the sins of the past and left us to fend for ourselves with our sins of the future?

Our consciences usually remain clear when life goes fairly smoothly and when we are able to stay out of trouble. But what happens when we fail and fall into sin? It needs to be made clear that it is possible for true Christians to fail. True believers can sometimes, in human weakness, commit the most appalling acts and do great harm to the gospel they espouse. Consider King David in the Old Testament. He committed adultery and murder. Or the apostle Peter in the New Testament who denied his Lord three times, a failure that caused him to weep bitterly.

It is probably right to point out that there is a vast difference between the true Christian who may fall because of the sinfulness and frailty of human nature and the constant testing of temptation and the hypocrite who makes great claims but habitually lives a life that is contrary to the gospel. There is a difference between the religious hypocrite and the sincere Christian who has to cope with the weakness of human nature. True Christians can, and do, sin. Some may even fall into gross sin, but most Christians struggle with sin in the ordinary everyday routine of living in a world that is hostile to God and His Son, Jesus Christ our Lord, and many do not cave in. They would not claim to be perfect or better than anyone else but they simply do not give in to all the temptations. They struggle with themselves and trust the power of the Holy Spirit living within them to give them grace to keep going every day and to endure the enemy's assaults.

But what happens when a believer does indeed succumb? What about these sins? When we do fail we are tempted to question our salvation. We ask ourselves, 'Am I really a Christian?' We doubt our justification and we lose our sense of peace. Some who fall experience unspeakable spiritual torment and agony of the soul. Inevitably we doubt our standing with God.

I do not wish to minimise the seriousness of sin and backsliding – especially by those who know better, those who have had the privilege of knowledge and understanding. All sin is a shameful thing and a backslidden Christian is a contradiction in terms. But we must understand our justification; our salvation is altogether and entirely dependent on what Christ did on the cross. It is in Him and because of Him that we are safe. It is *not* because of us or our actions in any way whatever. Thus, if you have been justified, you are justified once and for all. It is an irreversible act. Your behaviour may not always reflect your true standing with God, but your standing with God is not dependent on your behaviour but on Christ's act of atonement.

Look at it this way. If you say, 'I have sinned, therefore I have lost my salvation', you are in fact saying, 'I received my salvation because I was good'. We know this is not true. Thus, even when we fall into sin, it is nevertheless true, gloriously true, that we are still justified. This is surely grace upon grace.

This is a good place to remind you of the Bible's emphasis on the spiritual act of repentance. This means that there is a realization on our part that our actions are sinful and offensive to God. Recognizing that, we renounce our sinful actions; we turn away from them. More than that, we are appalled to think that such things could be part of our lives. When we become Christians, repentance is the conscious act we make against what we were and used to do. We change our minds about the value of those things. But as our Christian lives progress, we ourselves never progress beyond the need to repent. Repentance is a ready state of mind that is with us constantly. We engage in it every day. We are always repenting and saying 'Sorry' to God for our sins.

But the point here is that though I may still sin because I am fallen and weak, I never fall 'out' of the grace of God. And repentance and confession of sin is God's ordained way of re-establishing my conscious relationship with Him (1 John 1:8-9).

REGENERATION

I am well aware that this raises an enormous moral problem in the minds of some people. So let's face it and discuss it. Does this teaching that our justification means that all our sins – past, present and future – have been atoned for, leave us the possibility of living as we please because we will never be guilty again? Does it mean that future sins don't matter? Does it not open the door to careless and irresponsible thinking that suggests that we can do as we please and still get to heaven? The answer is a resounding *No!* I know that this is how some people have constructed this teaching on justification, but they are wrong. The great dimension which they forget is that when we are justified, we are also *regenerated*. That is another word for you to note. The word 'regenerated' means that we are made new. In other words our salvation does not merely have to do with the forgiveness of sins but also with the changing of our sinful natures. At justification a new instinct is placed within us. It is the instinct to be holy – like God.

I know that we can never be perfect as He is, and often our attempts at living righteously meet with defeat. But the point is that we have a new instinct, a new desire, because we have a new nature. We are 'in Christ' and Christ is 'in us'. The Holy Spirit comes to take up residence in our bodies and we experience new longings. Has this been your experience? Can you remember how thirsty you were to know more and more when you became a Christian? How sensitive you were to sin? How conscientiously you tried to change your behaviour patterns? Why? Because when you were justified, you were also regenerated. We use these terms separately to explain what has happened to us, but in practical terms they are part of one experience. Our experience of conversion may not be the same in every detail as someone else's as God works in different ways to accomplish what He pleases. But all true Christians have been justified by faith in the Lord Jesus Christ and regenerated – changed within. Their sins – past, present and future – have been forgiven and forgotten, forever!

If you are feeling down and defeated because of failure, get up again. You may be feeling cast down but God has not cast you out! You are justified. You are still His. Repent of your sin and remember that Jesus died for you. If you are feeling bad, you may well deserve to feel that way. But your salvation, your standing with God, does not depend on your feeling but on what Jesus did on Calvary. Remember that, believe it. It is the only way to blessed assurance.

Study Questions

Read Genesis 12:1-4, 15:1-6, Romans 4:18-25.

1. Discuss the link between Abraham's faith and ours (Romans 4:23-24).

2. Discuss the three elements of faith. To refresh your memory, read pp. 61-67.

3. Discuss the six tests of true faith mentioned in this chapter. (pp. 67-78)

4. Name three ways in which the old 'landlord' has tried to harass you. (pp. 70-71)

5. In what way is the experience of dying different for the Christian? (pp. 73-74)

6. If a Christian sins, does he forfeit his salvation? (pp. 76-77)

7. What is the difference between justification and regeneration? (p. 79)

8. What does the experience of regeneration mean for us in terms of daily living?

7

More on faith

I really want you to find complete assurance of salvation through faith in Christ. Yet I know that the very simplest act of all – faith or trust – can become the most difficult of all. The nineteenth-century preacher C.H. Spurgeon wrote:

> Faith is so simple a matter that, whenever I try to explain it, I am very fearful lest I should becloud its simplicity. When Thomas Scott had printed his notes upon *The Pilgrim's Progress*, he asked one of his parishioners whether she understood the book. 'Oh yes, sir,' said she, 'I understand Mr Bunyan very well enough, and I am hoping that one day, by divine grace, I may understand your explanations.' Should I not feel mortified if my reader should know what faith is, and then get confused by my explanation?

Likewise I can only hope and pray that you do not get confused by my explanations. However, as we conclude our discussion on this matter of faith or trust, I must make some additional comments.

TRUE FAITH

The first is a warning that, though faith is simple trust in Jesus, it is something that *the devil will attack* again and again. Often the simple act of trusting Jesus will have to fight for survival against doubt and accusation. You will find that, till the end of your days, your old enemy the devil will raise the issue of your justification. 'Are you sure you are really saved?' he will whisper. And his insidious suggestions will come at the most unexpected moments and in the most unlikely ways. You may find the battle to keep trusting in Jesus, the struggle for assurance, a desperate battle from time to time. But true spiritual faith will always win.

Remember that faith is a deliberate choice to believe God and trust what He says. And the very ability you have to make this choice is given to you by God. If He says your sins are forgiven and forgotten forever, that settles it. Believe it and rejoice.

Secondly, remember that true faith is always *more than mere intellectual assent*. There are many people who have no quarrel with what the Bible says, who truly believe every word, yet are not saved. Why not? Because their faith is nothing more than intellectual agreement with the facts. True saving faith is much more than that. It is to embrace willingly, humbly and trustingly all that Jesus has done for us. It is a personal appropriation of the great event of Christ's atoning death on the cross.

True faith leads to true joy – not merely positive thinking or lifting yourself into a psychological state of inner comfort by a process of elevated thought. It is a real peace brought about by justification – because our sins have been truly dealt with on the cross.

This leads me to a final observation. True Christian faith *never takes sin lightly*. It never trivialises sin. It cannot argue that, because God has justified us, we can live as we please. On the contrary, true faith longs to be free from sin, to be holy, to emulate the innocence of the Lord Jesus Christ. True Christian faith understands that a sense of assurance cannot be experienced until peace with God has been obtained. The man or woman who has true Christian faith has an understanding of the seriousness of judgement. They know that what Jesus endured on the cross was no less than hell itself. They are amazed at God's love for them and are therefore careful about the way they live. They are humble before God.

If this is the way you feel, then stop fretting. Peace is yours. Trust Him. Believe Him. Spurgeon reminds us that God has made the great necessities of life very simple matters. We must eat, therefore even a blind man can find his way to his mouth. We must drink and even the tiniest babe can do this without instruction. Faith is to spiritual things what eating and drinking are to temporal things. No one is so ignorant that they do not know how to eat or drink. Receive Him now; trust Him now. No effort is required from you except to reach out to Him in simple trust. And as you do so, you discover that God gives you the strength to trust more fully.

Late in 1944 a seventeen-year-old Russian boy was called up to fight in the war. By then the war was nearly over. He had no intention of risking his life at that late stage, so he hit on an idea. He prepared a hideout beneath a pigsty on the collective farm near the village of Ostrozhets in the Ukraine where he worked. He stocked up on food, furs and rugs. He arranged with his girlfriend to supply him with food and hot tea in the middle of the night. He arranged a farewell party and all his friends believed he was going to the front line. Instead he crept into his home-made cave and lived there – for the next thirty years! After a few months his girlfriend was transferred and he was left to fend for himself. He ate pigswill and foraged for food at night. He once had to stop gangrene spreading from a finger bitten by a pig by biting off the tip of his finger. When he finally emerged after many years, he was hunched over and almost unable to move. His skin had turned grey and he had lost most of his hair and teeth. But the worst was that he discovered that he had been granted amnesty by Stalin twenty-five years previously. How sad to live as a prisoner when, in fact, he was a free man.[1]

But so many Christians do this. You are free if you trust Christ. Do not live as a spiritual prisoner any more. The newspaper headlines read, 'Deserter didn't know of pardon'. But you *do* know. Enter now into the blessed assurance that Christ offers you by believing that His Word of forgiveness to you is true and put your trust in Him.

Study Questions

1. Suggest various ways in which your faith has been attacked.

2. Which of these options do you think is correct?

   Faith is:

   * a feeling that all is well
   * a decision to trust God's Word

   True faith is based on:

   * blind trust irrespective of the facts
   * an understanding of what Jesus did

---

1   *The Argus*, 17 December 1975.

3. Once again, choose the correct option. Discuss why you think your choice is correct.

   True faith leads to:
   - a carefree lifestyle
   - a carefulness in the way we live

8

Into All Blessing

There is more, much, much more, for those of us who have been justified by faith. Peace with God is the first of the great spiritual blessings that we receive. Now we turn to a second benefit. Paul says in Romans 5:2:

> ... through whom we have gained access by faith into this grace in which we now stand.

To understand this is to add to the sense of privilege and joy that belongs to all who have put their faith and trust in Jesus.

The first thing I want you to see clearly is what it is we have gained through Christ. The word used is 'access'. It is a word used only three times in the New Testament. Besides its use here, it also appears in Ephesians 2:18 and 3:12. This word is important for us to understand because it carries the sense of being introduced. The idea is that of being presented to a dignitary.

You have possibly been invited to a special formal occasion. We all know that we cannot simply gate-crash such events to meet important people. There are formalities to be observed. Procedures are necessary for us to gain access to the event. First, we must receive an invitation to which we must reply by a certain date. The dress code is probably indicated on the invitation. If we are to meet a very important person, we are met formally at the entrance of the venue and introduced to the dignitary.

These traditions of human society help us to understand our relationship with God. We cannot simply go into His presence. We need to be cleansed spiritually. Our own morality is as filthy rags. We need new 'clothes' – a robe of righteousness. These are the things that Jesus provided for us when we were justified. We may now be presented to the King dressed in our new righteousness.

There was a time when we had no right of entrance. But through Jesus we have gained access because of what He did on the cross and what God did for us when we put our trust in Jesus. He has obtained the credentials for us to be introduced to the Father. What Jesus did never needs to be repeated. It is done once for all.

Think of it in this way. The One who has the right of entry into the presence of God Himself now takes us by the hand and, with full confidence of His own acceptability, presents us to God the Father. It's almost as if He says, 'Father, meet John Smith. He has been washed in my blood. He is trusting in me to be reconciled to you'. And it's almost as if the Father warmly replies, 'I am so pleased to meet you. Anyone who has come to my Son for salvation is welcome in my house'.

I do not want to overstate or trivialise the meaning of scripture, but it seems as if this is the idea carried by the word 'access'. This is the second of the three blessings of justification. It is an introduction.

THIS GRACE

But an introduction to what? Note carefully the words in Romans 5:2. We have access or an introduction 'into this grace'. What does this mean? Here the word grace is used a little differently. The salvation which we receive from Christ is of such magnitude, so all-encompassing, that human words are inadequate to describe all its dimensions in one or two words.

The Bible therefore uses the same word to describe different dimensions of the same thing. In this case 'grace' does not refer primarily to the unmerited favour of God as it did previously, although that idea is certainly included. Here it refers to the new status we receive because we have been acquitted by God.

We are now in the realm where we are no longer guilty or condemned. It is a state of grace or a status of special blessing. Another way of putting it is to say that we have been introduced into a relationship with God in which we can receive certain benefits and blessings that we could not receive before. It is a dimension of living where we perpetually know the smile of God.

Previously we were rebels. We had no access into God's presence, nor did we deserve it. We were outside in the cold. We deserved nothing but judgement. Indeed, we were under judgement. But then came our justification. Now all has changed. Our sins have been paid for and God has pronounced us acquitted. We are in a position of favour. God accepts us, loves us, delights in us, receives us and pours out His blessings upon us. This is what the phrase 'this grace' means. This is what we have been introduced to. This is the access we have.

Let me illustrate it by referring to the well-known children's story of Cinderella. We know how she was miraculously transformed by her fairy godmother into a well-dressed young woman who could attend the prince's ball. We remember how she would once again become a poor peasant girl.

This is only a children's fairy tale but it serves to illustrate the privilege a Christian enjoys. Cinderella could lose all she had, all the status and splendour that went with being in the prince's presence. But we can never lose what we have. We have been transformed by grace into God's sons and daughters. We have a new status. We now live in 'this grace' where all God's blessings are available to us. For us there is no threatening stroke of twelve midnight, as there was for Cinderella. All we have from God is ours forever. It will never be taken away from us.

God's grace in saving us is free and undeserved. It is sheer mercy. And this state of grace into which we have been granted access is equally free and undeserved. It is all part of the great favour He bestows on those who deserve nothing but punishment.

To have access into 'this grace' means to have access to all that we could possibly need for the Christian life. That is why it is so futile to live with worry and to fear we may not have the strength to face trials. This grace is ours. Do we need consolation under a burden? It is ours because we are Christ's and Christ is God's.

WE NOW STAND

Notice the words at the end of Romans 5:2 '... in which we now stand'. It means to stand fast or firm. It underscores the finality and the absolute certainty of our new position in Christ. To stand implies stability and emphasises the security of our position in Christ.

Unlike Cinderella we shall never be out on the streets again. We stand secure and steady because God, by His grace, keeps those whom He has saved. We did not fall into grace and we cannot fall out of it. We were brought into His grace by God's sovereign power and He will keep us in it by His sovereign power.

There is no need to be unsure, unsteady, uncertain or fearful. You are not perfect any more than I am. We all make mistakes. You may sometimes be racked by doubt. But you must remember that you have been justified by God through faith in Christ. God has done something to you which He has promised never to revoke. You now have peace with God. You have been reconciled with Him.

As if that were not enough, you have been introduced, or given access, not only to salvation, but to this whole new status that belongs to those who belong to Christ – you have access into 'this grace'. You are in the place where God can bless you because you belong to Him. You only have to call to Him and He will answer you. He loves you and is delighted with you.

Furthermore, He undertakes to keep you so that you may 'stand' in this grace. There is no uncertainty about God's attitude towards you or about your ability to stand firm in the storms of life. He will keep you. You are in this place of unmerited, undeserved blessing for ever. And is this all? If it were, it would be overwhelming enough. But there is much more!

Study Questions

Read Romans 5:1-3 and Isaiah 64:6.

1. Discuss the difference in our status described in the two passages above.

2. In your own words, describe what the word 'access' means for you in your spiritual life. (p. 87)

3. Discuss the difference between receiving salvation by the grace of God and standing in the grace of God. (pp. 89-93)

4. What does the phrase 'standing in God's grace' mean to you in terms of spiritual security? (pp. 91-93)

5. Read Ephesians 1:1-14.

   - Identify the blessings that He gives us in Christ

   - List them and discuss them

   - Notice the word 'lavished' in verse 8

9

Hope

We now move on to the third area of blessing that results from justification. We have discussed peace with God and access into the realm of grace and blessing. Let us now look at *hope*. This sounds like a pretty ordinary word, but the Bible often uses words differently to the way we do. So many of our expressions have been devalued by misuse or slang over the years that the original meaning of many great words has been lost. The word 'hope' is one of these words. Let's look at Romans 5:2:

'And we rejoice in the hope of the glory of God.'

WE REJOICE

The first phrase we should note is 'And we rejoice'. Before we discuss what it is in which we rejoice, let us note how strong a word 'rejoice' is because it is part of what we ought to experience as Christians.

The word means 'to boast, exult or glory'. It's a word which contains the idea of being extremely pleased or satisfied by something either received or achieved.

Before his conversion Paul 'exulted' or 'boasted' in something else. He thought himself extremely righteous. He belonged to the strict Jewish sect known as the Pharisees. He thought that the strictness of his lifestyle and the constant observance of laws and rules made him pleasing to God. He puts it this way in Philippians 3:4-6:

> If anyone else thinks he has reason to put confidence in the flesh, I have more: circumcised on the eighth day, of the people of Israel, of the tribe of Benjamin, a Hebrew of Hebrews; in regard to the law, a Pharisee; as for zeal, persecuting the church; as for legalistic righteousness, faultless.

This is reinforced by his statement about his Christian life in Galatians 1:13-14:

> For you have heard of my previous way of life in Judaism, how intensely I persecuted the church of God and tried to destroy it. I was advancing in Judaism beyond many Jews of my own age, and was extremely zealous for the traditions of my fathers.

But when Paul became a Christian and experienced the liberating effect of being justified by faith in Jesus, instead of glorying in his own righteousness, he began to glory in Christ. He says in Galatians 6:14:

> May I never boast except in the cross of our Lord Jesus Christ, through which the world has been crucified to me, and I to the world.

He now exults in the cross of Jesus, the atoning sacrifice, the pardon of sin with all its glorious implications for the future. One way of describing the future implications of our salvation is the word *hope*. Thus Paul says in Romans 5:2:

> And we rejoice in the hope of the glory of God.

HOPE

The New Testament does not use the word *hope* the way we do today. We use the word to describe something that is uncertain. For instance, if a student is asked whether he has done well in the exams, he may say, 'I hope so', meaning that he can't be sure, he can only hope for the best.

It is used in exactly the opposite way in the New Testament. The word 'hope' does not refer to something uncertain, but rather to something definite and irrevocable. The word means that we look forward with certainty and confidence. It is a certainty which we anticipate.

In Titus 2:13 Paul describes the glorious appearing of our great God and Saviour Jesus Christ at His second coming as 'the blessed hope'. It's not uncertain – rather, it is the ultimate event for which we Christians wait. It *will* happen.

In Hebrews 6:19 the writer tells us that God's promise of salvation is so certain and sure that:

> We have this hope as an anchor for the soul, firm and secure.

Thus the word 'hope' implies that the outworking of our great salvation is something so certain and sure that we may exult or boast or rejoice in it. We *can* be happy and certain as Christians without being proud and presumptuous.

But what does this future, this 'hope,' consist of that makes us so joyful? What I am about to say is so important, so glorious, so profound in its implications that I feel inclined to ask you to stop reading at this point. Pause and pray that God will give you understanding of the great privilege you have and the great future that awaits you, so that you may never again doubt but rather be filled with blessed assurance.

Study Questions

Read Romans 5:2 (especially the last sentence), Romans 15:13, 2 Corinthians 4:16-18.

1. Is 'rejoicing' part of your spiritual experience?

2. Discuss the way we use the word 'hope' and contrast it with Titus 1:1-3.

3. What do you think is meant by the phrase 'anchor for the soul' in Hebrews 6:19?

4. Discuss what it is that we should be fixing our eyes on. (2 Cor. 4:18)

5. How does this view affect our involvement in this world?

   Refer to:
   - Matthew 25:31-46
   - Acts 20:35
   - 2 Corinthians 9:8
   - Philippians 2:12
   - 1 Thessalonians 2:9
   - 2 Thessalonians 3:10

10

The Glory of God

'... [A]nd we rejoice in the hope of the glory of God' (Rom. 5:2 ESV). How quickly we can read these words, yet how little they convey to us unless we pause to consider them. Let's ask the question, 'What do we mean by the glory of God?'

It's almost impossible to say very much about the subject of God's glory because of the limitations of human language. Our words are inadequate to convey any true sense of the glory of God. But this phrase refers to the essential nature of God, to the sum total of His excellences.

Think for a moment of some of the words the scriptures use to describe God: holy, righteous, faithful, good, love, light, merciful. The list goes on. All these words convey different aspects of His glory. The glory of God refers to the combination of all these excellences. Think about this for a moment. How holy is God? How righteous is He? How good? How loving? Who has ever understood? No wonder Paul cries out in Romans 11:33-36:

> Oh, the depth of the riches of the wisdom and knowledge of God! How unsearchable his judgements, and his paths beyond tracing out! Who has known the mind of the Lord? Or who has been his counsellor? Who has ever given to God, that God should repay him? For from him and through him and to him are all things. To him be the glory for ever! Amen.

He is holier and more righteous than we could ever imagine Him to be even though we contemplated His holiness for a thousand lifetimes. He is far above our thinking or estimation. Now take all His glorious excellences and combine them. We can still catch only the vaguest glimpse of His glory. The glory of God is the totality of all He is by His nature. In other words, all those attributes that make Him what He is by His nature constitute this glory.

So great and indescribable is His glory that the scriptures often refer to it in terms of brightness, radiance or light. All this has great bearing on our assurance. So let's look at some of the relevant passages in the Bible.

JESUS' GLORY

The first reference is found in Hebrews 1:3:

> The Son is the radiance of God's glory and the
> exact representation of his being, sustaining all
> things by his powerful word. After he had provid-
> ed purification for sins, he sat down at the right
> hand of the majesty in heaven.

Notice the phrase 'the radiance of God's glory'. This
implies a majesty, splendour and brightness. It refers to
a beauty which we cannot grasp. The idea of light is strong
when the Bible refers to God's glory. Read 1 John 1:5:

> This is the message we have heard from him and
> declare to you: God is light; in him there is no
> darkness at all.

Notice the phrase 'God is light; in him there is no
darkness at all'. This means that there is nothing
in God's character that can be construed as evil or
wrong. His innate goodness is expressed as light or
radiance. Next we refer to 2 Chronicles 7:1-3:

> When Solomon finished praying, fire came down
> from heaven and consumed the burnt offering
> and the sacrifices, and the glory of the Lord
> filled the temple. The priests could not enter
> the temple of the Lord because the glory of the
> Lord filled it. When all the Israelites saw the fire
> coming down and the glory of the Lord above the

> temple, they knelt on the pavement with their
> faces to the ground, and they worshipped and
> gave thanks to the Lord, saying, 'He is good: his
> love endures for ever'.

The word 'glory' is often used in the Old Testament
to describe the presence of God. In this moving
passage there are three particular things to notice
in regard to His glory. Firstly, God's glory is
equated with fire, radiance, brightness. Secondly,
so powerful was this visible expression of His
splendour that the people fell to their knees in awe
and adoration. Thirdly, this great experience left
the people with the overwhelming impression that
God is good, that His character is flawless. There
is that inherent quality in God that makes us know
instinctively that all He does is right and all His
actions are benevolent.

Now move to the story of Jesus' birth as record-
ed in Luke 2. In verse 14 we read of an amazing
event witnessed by the shepherds. A great company
of heavenly beings called angels burst into song of
'glory to God' at the birth of Jesus. The great praise
due to Him as a glorious person is sung by glorious
beings. Glorious though they are, they pay hom-
age to One whose glory far outshines theirs and of
whose glory their own is only a pale, though wonderful, reflection. There are other references to
Christ's glory in the gospels. In John 1:14 we read:

> We have seen his glory, the glory of the One and only,
> who came from the Father, full of grace and truth.

What was John referring to? There are several New Testament references to Christ's glory. You may remember the amazing event at His baptism when the Holy Spirit descended upon Him and the Father's voice was heard affirming Jesus:

> This is my Son, whom I love; with him I am well pleased. (Matt 3:17)

That was an indication of Jesus' great stature in the eyes of His Father. In Matthew 17:2 we have the account of our Lord's transfiguration. Peter, James and John saw His face shining like the sun and His clothes became as white as the light. But this is not all.

- Stephen, the first Christian martyr, saw the glory of Jesus (Acts 7:55).

- Saul of Tarsus, the apostle Paul, saw it on the road to Damascus. Luke tells us in Acts 9:3: '... a light from heaven flashed around him'.

- In 2 Corinthians 12 Paul tells us of a mysterious experience he had of being caught up to heaven and hearing inexpressible things.

What are we to make of these things? Are they simply mystical, biblical references to make us feel as if true spirituality is out of reach? *No!* They are written for our comfort, to give us assurance, to promote our inner certainty and confidence. Why? Because one day all who know Christ can expect to join together to behold His glory.

In this world we live by faith, not by sight. How often we long for visible evidence of the things we believe. We wish that God would reveal Himself to us in a special way so that our fears could be quelled and we could be assured. But this is not the norm. Here we live by faith. But the great promise is that one day we will see Him and witness His glory.

Our hearts will be overwhelmed by the greatness of the light. We will rejoice again in His radiant presence. We ourselves, our struggles finally over, will stand in the presence of God and see with our own eyes the glory of God and of Christ. There will no longer be a veil over our eyes. We will not need faith then, for we will see Him as He is. We will be face to face with Him in heaven. The apostle John puts it like this in Revelation 5:13-14 where he describes the scene in heaven:

> Then I heard every creature in heaven and on earth and under the earth and on the sea, and all that is in them, singing: 'to him who sits on the throne and to the Lamb be praise and honour and glory and power for ever and ever!' The four living creatures said, 'Amen', and the elders fell down and worshipped.

OUR GLORIFICATION

But this is not all. The best is yet to come. Our hope is not merely that our struggles will be over one day and we will see Him. That is wonderful enough, but there is more. We will not only see His glory, but we will *share* it. We ourselves will be glorified. We will not remain in this weak and limited state. Rather, when Jesus returns and the great resurrection takes place, we will be changed and we will have glorious bodies like His (John 5:28-30, Rom.8:18, 29-30, 1 Cor. 15:50-51, 1 John 3:1-3).

This part of our salvation is called our 'glorification'. This is the hope Paul had in mind. This is what we are promised when we are justified. How unspeakable and indescribable is God's grace.

Look at it in this way. Adam and Eve enjoyed God's presence in Eden. They were perfect, sinless. They were required only to obey God. What would have happened if they had not sinned? In all likelihood they would have been blessed and promoted into the state of glory that we are told awaits the children of God.

We were created for the purpose of sharing in the glory of God. But Adam did sin and this great privilege was forfeited for the human race. That is why the scriptures say:

> ... for all have sinned and fall short of the glory of God ... . (Rom. 3:23)

We were meant for glory but did not attain to it. It was lost because in Adam we all fell short of God's standard. But the gospel tells us that this glory is restored to us in Christ. We are going to possess it again. Read what Paul says in Philippians 3:21:

> ... who, by the power that enables him to bring everything under his control, will transform our lowly bodies so that they will be like his glorious body.

'Our lowly bodies' will be transformed into what? Into the likeness of His glorious body! Yes, agrees John:

> ... we shall be like him, for we shall see him as he is. (1 John 3:2)

What grace! What mercy! What power! We shall see Jesus as He is. Even more – we shall be like Him!

OUR HOPE

That is the Christian's possession – hope. This is why we are able to rejoice and exalt. We may feel that we have a long way to go, but we don't lose heart. God is changing us day by day. Our final glorification is a happy certainty, a blessed hope for all who have been justified by faith.

This has bearing on the healing movements of today. While we rejoice to know that God can and does on occasion answer our prayers for physical healing, we need to realise that the focus of the Bible is on our ultimate glorification when all weakness and sickness will be removed. The frantic search for physical miracles is partly the result of Christians not understanding the Bible's teaching about the plan and purpose of God for His people. His plan is for us to be ultimately glorified. Until then, we continue to live in an imperfect world in which Christians do not escape tribulation and trial.

I urge you not to give up. Do not feel that God has deserted you because He has not answered your prayers for relief in some affliction. Do not listen to well-meaning friends who insist that you do not have enough faith. God's will for you is first and foremost your spiritual growth. Your affliction may be part of the process. When you were justified, you were introduced to a whole new realm of grace. You can exult, glory and rejoice in this special possession – the hope of the glory of God in which you will one day share.

These things make up your certainty and assurance. How can you rejoice if your final glorification depends on you? No, it is all of God, all of grace. It is yours for ever because it is bestowed on you by God.

Do not dwell on your weakness or brood over your failures. Do not listen to the world or its threats. Do not pay attention to the irresponsible statements of ignorant Christians. It is all of God, all by faith. Look to the person of Jesus. See the glory there. That glory awaits *you!* Yes, even you!

Study Questions

1. Discuss what the phrase 'the glory of God' means. (p. 101)

2. Discuss the following Bible passages:
   - Matthew 17:2
   - Hebrews 1:3
   - 1 John 1:5

   What is the common denominator used to describe the glory of God? (p. 102)

3. Why will our hearts one day be overwhelmed by the greatness of the 'light'? (p. 106)

4. What does the word 'glorification' mean? (p. 107)

5. What was it that was lost when Adam sinned? (pp. 107-108)

6. Read Romans 3:23. What does it mean to fall short of the glory of God? Compare the 'all' of this verse with the 'all' of verse 12 above.

7. The Christian believer can look forward with confidence to something certain and sure. What is it? (p. 108)

11

When Things Go Wrong

I want to return to the on-going search for physical healing we touched on at the end of the previous chapter. While most people may be moved at the general suffering in the world, for many others the picture of worldwide suffering and misery is eclipsed by their personal search for health and healing.

Crowds still throng to various pilgrimage sites around the world in the hope of a special touch from God. Preachers who claim to have special healing ministries still draw crowds of people. In spite of exposures of fraud and dishonesty, trickery or exaggerated claims, the stories of many people who were not healed and the near impossibility of finding any reliable verification of those who claim to be healed, the crowds press on in the hope that something miraculous will happen.

The Christian and healing

In some circles, if anyone dares to suggest that the healing movement is based on wrong presuppositions, that person is quickly marginalized. It appears that, in some quarters, the new criteria by which we measure religious orthodoxy are no longer the scriptures but rather the personal opinion of the individual concerning religious experiences, charismatic phenomena and physical healing.

However, with great sensitivity to many sincere believers, I have to say that the search and the demand for healing are based on certain fundamental misunderstandings regarding the role of suffering in the life of the Christian. 'What!' some may exclaim, 'Does suffering and affliction actually have a role to play?' The answer is a most decisive yes. This flies directly in the face of much of today's teaching that sickness is of the devil and that spiritual victory and physical health are their constant experience. Victory, in this context, usually refers to freedom from sickness or disaster of any kind.

This in turn has given rise to bizarre practices found among some Christians such as rebuking illnesses, rebuking circumstances, rebuking certain sins or rebuking the devil. This personification of illness and circumstances stems from the belief that the devil is behind all suffering. Further, they take our Lord's rebuking of the devil in the New Testament as a model for normal Christian practice today whereas His miracles were intended to validate His claim to be the Son of God by demonstrating His amazing authority over demons, sickness and even the natural elements.

However, this book is not a discussion about the validity of miracles. Suffice to say that all Christians believe in the supernatural power of God and His ability to perform miracles whenever He pleases. All Christians also believe it is their bounden duty to bring the sick and suffering before God in prayer. In that way we leave them to His grace and mercy – a very different thing from demanding and claiming healing miracles.

Sometimes God heals and sometimes He doesn't. The purpose of this part of the book is to seek to understand why He doesn't. What is He saying to us when He allows the afflictions of life to come upon us without any form of external relief? Is there a purpose to suffering? Yes, there is, and especially so for the Christian.

This book is aimed at helping Christians to rediscover the joy and thrill of being children of God. Why are we not filled with joy? Precisely because we have not understood the great themes in the Bible which explain God's relationship to us and our life in this world, fallen and broken as it is. Instead of humbly hearing and believing God's

Word, we have been deluded by a form of mysticism that has invaded the lives of many Christians.

This new form of believing takes us into the realm of emotion, experiences, dreams, visions and so called supernatural intervention, even in the very mundane things of life. I have even heard Christians rebuking the devil when their car won't start!

The problem with this kind of behaviour is that it leaves enormous questions when it doesn't work. Inevitably the believer blames himself. He seeks a reason in himself why God did not respond to his prayers or his 'faith'. Many sincere and well-meaning people have been plunged into spiritual despair as a result. Some have concluded that they are either guilty of a sin which has yet to be revealed to them or they have failed to muster enough faith. Whatever it may be, they feel a spiritual failure.

How is it possible to live daily in the knowledge of God's love if we constantly feel a sense of God's disapproval? We can't! This sense of failure and despair is wrong because it stems from a wrong view of the role and the purpose of suffering.

THE CHRISTIAN AND SUFFERING
How could Paul write 'but we also rejoice in our suffering' (Rom. 5:3)? Rather than being something that is always from the devil, suffering is often the way God uses to give us further proof that we

belong to Him. It is a way of confirming that we are destined for that glory which awaits us. This affirmation comes to us because of the way our faith enables us to face the trials, troubles and tribulations of life.[1]

When we look for evidence of spiritual reality in someone's life, we often look for things God does not look for. We are impressed by testimonies, personal skills and abilities, how successful they have been in sharing their faith and so on. But one of the most subtle and important tests of the reality of our commitment to Jesus is the way we react to trouble. This is probably the starkest difference between the believer and the unbeliever.

When a person who is not a Christian encounters the trials and tragedies of life, he has no answer for them. It is all a mystery. In fact, life itself is a mystery. He can usually cope while all goes well, but when the unexpected happens or tragedy strikes, there is nothing to say. The clever philosophies by which people live in good days fall apart in the face of affliction. Often the unbelieving man or woman can do nothing but look at the difficulties of their lives and say with Shakespeare: 'How full of briars is this working day world.'

We must re-establish the fact that trials, tribulations and suffering do not disappear when we

---

1   See pp. 118-22.

become Christians. Rather they become a vital and on-going test of our Christian profession. The Bible is full of evidence of the suffering and the afflictions of those who trust in God. How then should the Christian react when suffering overtakes him?

Christians should remember that there are *different kinds of suffering* in the world. There are, for instance, the ordinary trials that most of us face simply because we are human beings living in a broken world. We marry, get caught up in family conflicts, grow old, weak or sickly. These are some of the things that burden most of us. Life is rarely an uninterrupted flow of happiness and contentment.

Then there are the afflictions of war and tragedy that affect many Christians. Trapped between the crossfire of warring factions in a conflict they did not want and have not engineered, many true believers are killed, maimed and injured. If it is not war, it may be drought, earthquakes or floods. Christians suffer in the same way as everyone else.

On a more personal level, Christians sometimes face the heartbreak of a failed marriage or the loss of a loved one. Sometimes they have to carry the burden of a terminal illness. When these things happen, the enormity of the tragedy is personal. The misfortunes of others seem to pale into insignificance. Our minds are blocked by our own sadness and misery so that we cannot concentrate on others.

I do not want to give the impression that Christians have no special resources to call on in time of need. Many Christians have experienced the keeping and protecting power of God during such times. Of course all Christians have the right to call on their heavenly Father. In fact, they are specially urged to do so to obtain help:

> Let us then approach the throne of grace with confidence, so that we may receive mercy and find grace to help us in our time of need. (Heb. 4:16)

We must remember that suffering is part and parcel of living in a fallen world. However, the suffering that Paul was referring to in Romans 5:3 is probably the suffering that comes upon us simply because we are Christians. It is a reference to the hardships, discrimination and persecution we have to endure as we strive to live for Christ. This is reinforced by his comments in Romans 8:17:

> Now if we are children, then we are heirs – heirs of God and co-heirs with Christ, if indeed we share in his sufferings in order that we may also share in his glory.

Our Lord Himself warned us that, as He was rejected, so would we be. In Matthew 5:10-12 Jesus went as far as to say that those who suffer for His name are blessed:

> Blessed are those who are persecuted because of righteousness, for theirs is the kingdom of heaven. Blessed are you when people insult you, persecute you and falsely say all kinds of evil against you because of me. Rejoice and be glad, because great is your reward in heaven, for in the same way they persecuted the prophets who were before you.

To experience rejection of any sort because you are a Christian is to be placed in the company of the prophets of old. It is a sign that you belong to God and that His Holy Spirit is in you. The Christian's attitude to suffering is thus not merely a stoical attitude of endurance or an exercise of courage. Rather it is a positive attitude of rejoicing to know that we are true children of God. The Christian attitude is governed by an understanding of suffering that the non-Christian does not have. He knows certain things about suffering that are hidden from the unbeliever.

RESULTS OF SUFFERING

Certain things produced by suffering cannot be obtained in any other way. The first positive result of suffering that Paul mentions is *perseverance*. This is an element of Christian character which is produced and refined in the furnace of suffering. It refers to that constancy and steadfastness which is so needed today when old virtues are being eroded in the present climate of personal pleasure and comfort. What we are referring to here is not a mere natural steadfastness but rather a supernatural ability imparted by the Holy Spirit. Some people have a stubborn nature that is part of their temperament. This is not what is meant by the steadfastness. By virtue of our natural temperament we may not be able to hold out and be steadfast. When difficulties come, we realise that we have no one to turn to but the Lord. Trouble and trials therefore cast us upon the Lord. We are driven to our knees in prayer and made to depend on Him and Him alone.

Trouble has a way of helping us to get to know ourselves as we note how we behave under pressure. It examines us and shows up our flaws, weaknesses and strengths. It highlights whether we have true saving faith or not, whether we are the true children of God or whether our faith is superficial and false.

But there is more. Paul tells us that this kind of perseverance, constancy or steadfastness has its own result. It in turn produces *character*. This refers to an 'approvedness'. Our steadfastness in the face of suffering is evidence to us and to others that we are real Christians. It signifies that we have passed the test. It highlights the fact that we have spiritual integrity and underscores the words of James 1:12:

Blessed is the man who perseveres under trial, because when he has stood the test, he will receive the crown of life that God has promised to those who love him.

It proves the truth of 1 Peter 1:7:

These have come so that your faith – of greater worth than gold, which perishes even though refined by fire – may be proved genuine and may result in praise, glory and honour when Jesus Christ is revealed.

Your faith has been proved genuine. It is of greater worth than gold. Why? Because it is real saving faith. It assures you of your eternal destiny. It develops character.

Suffering also tests our love for God. Often when we go through difficult times the devil whispers, 'Does God really love you?' True Christian character has no doubt about that. Not only are we sure of our love for Him, not only do we love Him when all is going well; we love Him at all times. We have access to Him. We know that we are at peace with Him. We are headed for glory. Therefore we do not panic when troubles come. We rest in the knowledge that He is ours and we are His.

This character that forms in us as we steadfastly continue to trust Him has its own result – hope. What does this mean? As we consistently trust God, as we pass the test of faith and develop character, so the evidence that we are heirs of glory mounts up in our hearts and minds. Our assurance and our dependence on Him increase. We know that we are going to glory. We know that even the furnace of affliction is in His hand and He is our Father. He has started the process of purifying us, and He will continue it until He calls us home.

Our suffering and trials make us even surer that we are His. They drive us back to God, His strength, His sufficiency. We rest in His purposes for us and His loving concern for us. We agree with the psalmist when he says in Psalm 119:71:

> It is good for me to be afflicted so that I might learn your decrees.

When the trial has passed we are often able to say, 'I am better than I was before. I am more certain of God, more certain of my relationship to Him, more certain of His love for me, more certain of the love of the Lord Jesus Christ.'

Thus our faith enables us to view suffering in such a way that we can see that, far from evidence that God has forgotten us, it proves that He is very much at work in our lives, promoting our holiness and preparing us for heaven. We find ourselves agreeing with the writer to the Hebrews 12:11:

> No discipline seems pleasant at the time, but
> painful. Later on, however, it produces a harvest
> of righteousness and peace for those who have
> been trained by it.

This hope is most certainly not empty or hollow. There is no disappointment in this hope. It is not futile or pointless. Part of our certainty of this glorious future lies in the assurance the Holy Spirit gives us of the love of God. This blessed third Person of the Trinity comes to indwell us, uniting us to Christ and pouring out God's love in our hearts. He is an inner witness to the reality of our justification, acceptance and final glory. It is an assurance in the inner depths of our being – our soul, or spirit, that part of us where we react spiritually. There God pours out His love by His Spirit to assure us that His salvation is real and irreversible.

Do you have this salvation? Have you crumbled under suffering? Get up again. Go to God – ask for grace to endure, to see that you are His. Submit to God's wisdom. Let true Christian character be formed in you. Ask the Holy Spirit to pour out the evidence of God's love in your heart. Learn to rejoice – yes, even in your suffering.

Study Questions

1. Tick your answer.

    Suffering, afflictions and illnesses and personal tragedy produce:

    - a sense that God does not love me
    - a sense that this world is not my final home
    - a feeling of guilt because of lack of faith

    Why do you feel the way you do?

    Read Psalm 119:67, 71.

2. List some of the sources of suffering mentioned on p. 116. Discuss them to see if they are applicable to Christians.

3. What is the special source of suffering experienced by Christians in this world? (pp. 117-18)

    Read Matthew 5:10-12.

4. Discuss some of the ways in which suffering benefits us spiritually. (pp. 118-22)

    Refer to Hebrews 12:4-13.

12

The Holy Spirit: gift of assurance

In Romans 5:5 Paul refers to '... the Holy Spirit, whom he has given us.' This underscores the great and comforting truth that the Holy Spirit of God is given to all Christians.

RECEIVING THE SPIRIT

We must resist the tendency to make the receiving of the Holy Spirit – the 'filling' of the Spirit – dependent on an experience after conversion. Although a Christian may have many special experiences of the Holy Spirit after conversion, it is nevertheless at the moment of conversion that the Spirit takes up residence in us. Paul reinforces his argument in Romans 8:9-11:

> You, however, are controlled not by the sinful nature but by the Spirit, if the Spirit of God lives

in you. And if anyone does not have the Spirit of Christ, he does not belong to Christ. But if Christ is in you, your body is dead because of sin, yet your spirit is alive because of righteousness. And if the Spirit of him who raised Jesus from the dead is living in you, he who raised Christ from the dead will also give life to your mortal bodies through his Spirit, who lives in you.

In other words our new life in Christ is sometimes described as new birth. In Acts 19:2 conversion is equated with 'receiving the Spirit'. We should remember the Holy Spirit is not merely an influence but a Person. He is the third Person in the Trinity and He has been given to us as the great gift of Jesus to His people. He is the Comforter Jesus said would come in His place (John 14:16-26).

The astonishing fact is that this wonderful, divine Person takes up residence in our bodies:

Do you not know that your body is a temple of the Holy Spirit, who is in you, whom you have received from God? You are not your own; you were bought at a price. Therefore honour God with your body. (1 Cor. 6:19-20)

Why does this happen? What is the purpose of the indwelling work of the Spirit? The indwelling of the Spirit is proof that we have experienced the new birth. The gift of the new birth is always the work of the Holy Spirit. He grants us spiritual enlightenment. He places the desire for salvation in our hearts, grants understanding of the significance of Christ's death on the cross and frees us to place our faith in Christ. Regeneration takes place first, and then the Spirit comes to indwell us. From the point of view of our experience, this all happens at the same time. But it is helpful to remember the sequence of divine activity in our lives.

The fact that the Holy Spirit takes up residence within us is intended as a guarantee from God of the finality of our eternal salvation. He is intended by God to be a gift of assurance to fill us with certainty and joy in believing.

Why are so many Christians defeated and miserable? One reason is that they have not understood the gospel properly in the sense that they have failed to recognise the privileges that are theirs. Because of this, they are constantly seeking more evidence that they are in fact Christians. They are easily led into the murky waters of emotional and mystical experiences with all the uncertainties and disillusionment that accompany them. You need no more than Christ, the Bible and simple faith in the gospel to become an assured child of God. Look at Ephesians 1:13-14:

> And you also were included in Christ when you heard the word of truth, the gospel of your

salvation. Having believed, you were marked in him with a seal, the promised Holy Spirit, who is a deposit guaranteeing our inheritance until the redemption of those who are God's possession – to the praise of his glory.

GUARANTEED AND SEALED

Look particularly at the words: 'Having believed, you were marked in him with a seal, the promised Holy Spirit, who is a deposit guaranteeing our inheritance.' We are told two amazing things about the Holy Spirit. Firstly, He is a *deposit guaranteeing our inheritance.*

We are all familiar with the procedure of entering into hire-purchase agreements. An agreement is drawn up and a deposit is made. That deposit is meant to be your guarantee that you will pay the rest of the amount owing on the item purchased. In fallen human society, things often do not work that way. People sometimes renege on their agreements. But this is, nevertheless, what Paul has in mind in this passage.

God intends the presence of the Holy Spirit in our lives to be a deposit, a first instalment guaranteeing that the rest – our eternal and heavenly inheritance – is yet to come and will most certainly come. The Holy Spirit brings with Him new power for us to draw on, divine impulses operating within us. He is the first instalment of glory to come.

But a second truth about the Holy Spirit is mentioned. He is described as a 'seal'. This is a reference to the *stamp of ownership* that a merchant might put on a bag of his merchandise, much as we might see in any industrial warehouse today. Having believed in Jesus, we are told we have received a mark, a seal. An ownership emblem has been placed on us.

The owner is God and the seal or mark is the Holy Spirit. We belong to God and nothing can alter that. All those who truly trust Christ are God's. They are safe in His hands. God now places a sign on them to indicate that they are His. That sign is the presence of the Holy Spirit. He indwells us, not only to assure us that there is more to come, but also to mark us out as God's own property. It is God's way of saying, 'You are mine. You have been redeemed by my Son. You belong to me and, although my plan for you may include many ups and downs, I guarantee to complete all that has begun until you are safe in my presence.'

The Holy Spirit's presence in your life guarantees that you will grow more and more into His likeness. That is the mark – Christ-likeness. The seal of ownership is nothing less than the blessed third Person of the Holy Trinity indwelling our lives.

He guarantees the work of God in your soul and He is the proof that such a work of God cannot disappear or be destroyed. You cannot fall out of God's hands. You cannot fall out of God's grace, because you cannot fall out of God's plan. His plan is made. It is steadfast and immutable. You cannot be a Christian one day and not the next. Such thinking indicates that you have not understood clearly the grace of God.

The Holy Spirit in your life is a guarantee that, despite your weakness, you truly belong to God and you *will* continue in the faith. You need not fear that you will not last the pace. Left to yourself you certainly will not. But Christians are not left to themselves. They have a great Helper sent by their great Friend and Saviour. He ensures that we will have the strength to keep going.

Left to myself I have no hope because I am lazy, forgetful, weak and frail, and I love the world too much. But the Holy Spirit in me places holy desires in my heart. He makes me willing to obey God. He influences me, checks me, encourages me and rebukes me. He guides me and directs my heart and mind to true godliness. He gives me enlightenment and understanding. He works in me to cleanse away sin so that one day I will be presented before God:

> ... without stain or wrinkle or any other blemish, but holy and blameless. (Eph. 5:27)

Through prayer the Holy Spirit enables me to stay in touch with God. He is my deposit and my seal of ownership. Every change in me for the better is further proof that I belong to God. Let us stop our moping and misery. Let us believe these things and truly begin to enjoy our walk with God.

Study Questions

Read Romans 8:9-11.

1. Discuss the difference between the view that the Holy Spirit is merely an influence upon our lives and the view that He is a Person who lives in us. Refer to 1 Corinthians 6:19-20.

2. What does the Holy Spirit indwelling us prove? (pp. 126-7)

   Read 1 Corinthians 12:3.

3. Discuss what it means to have the Holy Spirit as a 'deposit' and a 'seal' in your life. (p. 128)

   Read Ephesians 1:13-14.

13

The Holy Spirit within

How can we know that the Holy Spirit has been given to us? It is usually a self-evident fact that, when you are a Christian, you are changed in such a way that you can only exclaim, 'To God be the Glory!' However, there are many sincere and anxious people who are filled with doubt about themselves and their standing before God. They often long to know for sure that they are saved but feel unable to make that assessment. They have no confidence in their spiritual experience. Are you perhaps one of these people? Rest assured that God cares about you even in your doubt.

The way to obtain assurance that you are justified and that the Spirit has been given to you is twofold. In the first place you must call upon God unceasingly to bring His own evidence to bear on your mind and emotions. Some people by way of temperament are always unsure of themselves. *Prayer* is the first and most important way forward.

Call on God, trusting in the merit of the Lord Jesus Christ. Tell Him that you believe the gospel and that you long to feel the gospel in your heart. Ask Him to pour out His love in your soul and to give you an inner witness that you have received the Spirit.

The second way to test whether the Holy Spirit has been given to you is to ask yourself certain 'gospel questions'. Examine yourself by *asking questions* that reveal what you think about Jesus Christ, the way of salvation and the fruits of the Christian faith. The cumulative answers are usually a good indication that you are a true Christian.

QUESTIONS TO CONSIDER

DO YOU ACKNOWLEDGE THAT JESUS CHRIST IS LORD OF ALL CREATION?

This does not mean the mere uttering of words. Anybody can do that. We witness that in many churches like my own where the Apostles' Creed may be regularly recited. Great gospel statements are sometimes uttered without any impact on the lives of those speaking them. Acknowledging Jesus as Lord implies a total commitment of yourself to the teaching of the New Testament concerning the

Person of Christ. This means that we accept that He was truly man and truly God. He has two natures in one Person. This is a great mystery. The incarnation of Christ brought about this amazing fact. He is truly God, truly man. He was Jesus of Nazareth, a carpenter's son, but He is also Christ, Son of the living God. He was human, became weary and fell asleep in a boat, but He also rebuked the winds and the waves and they became calm.

Jesus is the creator of the universe, yet also the Saviour of sinners. He went to the cross and shed His blood. He bought me, ransomed me and paid the price of my deliverance by His substitutionary death on the cross. His person, His work, His life, His death, burial, resurrection, His ascension and exaltation at the right hand of God and the promise of His second coming are all true. Jesus is *Lord*.

Do you believe this? Are these things of vital importance to you? Do you understand, even if not with all the clarity that you would like, that these things are essential for your salvation? Have you understood that you cannot save yourself? Have you given up trusting yourself and entrusted your eternal future to Jesus? If so, hear what the scriptures say in 1 Corinthians 12:3:

> … no-one can say, 'Jesus is Lord,' except by the Holy Spirit.

Do not be doubting, but believing. Thank God for opening your eyes. No one can believe these things sincerely unless the Holy Spirit is in them. There are other questions you can ask yourself. Turn to 1 John 1:6:

> If we claim to have fellowship with him yet walk in the darkness, we lie and do not live by the truth.

HAVE YOU STOPPED SINNING?

I am not asking whether you have become perfect, but rather if the tendency to sin has been arrested. Has the direction of your life changed? If you have been involved in blatant wrongdoing, has it stopped? You may not be perfect but, if after believing in Jesus, your repentance has resulted in a lifestyle that is changing every day, that is a sure sign that you have been given the Holy Spirit. Still in this vein, turn to 1 John 2:9 and 4:20-21:

> Anyone who claims to be in the light but hates his brother is still in the darkness.

> If anyone says, 'I love God,' yet hates his brother, he is a liar. For anyone who does not love his brother, whom he has seen, cannot love God, whom he has not seen. And he has given us this commandment: Whoever loves God must also love his brother.

DO YOU LOVE OTHER CHRISTIANS?

I do not mean, can you give blanket approval to all
that other Christians do? Rather, do you find your
heart knitted together with others who love Jesus?
Do you long to be in fellowship with other believers?
Are you willing to do what you can by way of serving
them, helping them and encouraging them? That is
more evidence of a new life. Read 1 John 2:15:

> Do not love the world or anything in the world.
> If anyone loves the world, the love of the Father
> is not in him.

DO YOU FIND YOURSELF BECOMING MORE AND MORE IN-DEPENDENT OF WHAT YOUR FRIENDS THINK ABOUT YOU?

Do you feel the pressure of the world and its godless
opinions losing their grip on you? That is yet more
evidence to assure you – a tell-tale sign that God has
given you the Holy Spirit. In 1 John 5:2-3 we read:

> This is how we know that we love the children
> of God: by loving God and carrying out his com-
> mands. This is love for God: to obey his commands.
> And his commands are not burdensome …

DO YOU LOVE GOD?

If you love God, you will love Christ. Do you love
Christ? Do you find a new instinct within you to
obey Him? Those who truly belong to Him do what
He says. Read John 14:21:

> Whoever has my commands and obeys them, he
> is the one who loves me. He who loves me will
> be loved by my Father, and I too will love him and
> show myself to him.

Loving Him means embracing His teachings and
obeying His will as far as we can discern it. Is this
true in your life? Turn now to Galatians 5:22-23:

> But the fruit of the Spirit is love, joy, peace, patience,
> kindness, goodness, faithfulness, gentleness and
> self-control. Against such things there is no law.

In this famous passage we have some of the evidence
of the presence of the Spirit in our lives. These are
the characteristics of one who has been given the
Spirit. The Holy Spirit reproduces the character of
Jesus in us.

DO YOU SEE THESE QUALITIES IN YOURSELF?

You may not see them perfectly, or even clearly —
but are they there? Are they becoming part of your
mind-set?

These are some of the questions we can ask and
some of the biblical tests we can apply. But I must
reiterate that only God can give us assurance and we
must ask for it.

Study Questions

1. What is meant by 'gospel questions'? (pp. 133-4)
   Can you pass the 'gospel question' test? (p. 134)

2. Discuss the following Bible passages:
   - 1 John 1:6
   - 1 John 2:9
   - 1 John 4:20-21

   How do you react to these statements?

3. What does the phrase 'love the world' mean in
   1 John 2:15? Have you experienced a change in
   yourself in regard to the 'world'?

4. Read 1 John 5:2-3. Do you feel this way about
   God? Compare this with our Lord's words in
   John 14:21.

5. Read Galatians 5:22-23. Are you able to discern
   the beginnings of these fruits in your life?

Conclusion

God expects us to believe what His Word says about us and the salvation He has provided. God will not work outside His Word. If you do not believe what He says in His Word, He will not provide any special assurance just for you.

This short study of selected passages from Romans is designed to help us understand how great our salvation is, how definite it is, how sure and certain because it is rooted in the character of the God of all truth who cannot lie. We must believe in His Word.

How sad to be uncertain and unsure of our salvation when we are meant to enjoy it, boast and exult in it. We are meant to anticipate the glory of God in which we will share. We have a great and sure inheritance.

These passages from Romans remind us that all three Persons of the blessed Trinity are interested and involved in our salvation. Shame on us for being so lethargic and negative! We need to humble ourselves before God and worship Him with praise and adoration.

'Therefore, since we have been justified through faith, we have peace with God through our Lord Jesus Christ ...' (Rom. 5:1).

Assurance

How to know you are a Christian

J.C. RYLE

ASSURANCE
How to know you are a Christian

J.C. RYLE

ISBN 9781871676051

It is right to have confidence in your Christian life, if that confidence stems from God's saving power. J.C. Ryle shows us that assurance is something every Christian should desire. There are steps we can take in our search for that goal; these are clearly marked out for us by Ryle. Do you know that you are part of God's family?

J. C. Ryle (1816-1900) was the first Bishop of Liverpool. He was one of the most authoritative churchmen of his time and his writings have been in constant demand throughout the last hundred years. His popularity was due to his clear and simple style, his longevity due to his being a profound thinker and compassionate pastor.

Christian Focus Publications

Our mission statement –

STAYING FAITHFUL

In dependence upon God we seek to impact the world through literature faithful to His infallible Word, the Bible. Our aim is to ensure that the Lord Jesus Christ is presented as the only hope to obtain forgiveness of sin, live a useful life and look forward to heaven with Him.

Our Books are published in four imprints:

CHRISTIAN FOCUS

popular works including biographies, commentaries, basic doctrine and Christian living.

CHRISTIAN HERITAGE

books representing some of the best material from the rich heritage of the church.

MENTOR

books written at a level suitable for Bible College and seminary students, pastors, and other serious readers. The imprint includes commentaries, doctrinal studies, examination of current issues and church history.

CF4•K

children's books for quality Bible teaching and for all age groups: Sunday school curriculum, puzzle and activity books; personal and family devotional titles, biographies and inspirational stories – Because you are never too young to know Jesus!

Christian Focus Publications Ltd,
Geanies House, Fearn, Ross-shire,
IV20 1TW, Scotland, United Kingdom.
www.christianfocus.com